Praise for

Song *of my* Soul

Song of my Soul is a gripping and emotional account of an Estonian refugee family's journey, set against the backdrop of the dramatic events of the Second World War. Rakfeldt's reflections on his upbringing in the U.S. while wrestling with his dual identity are humorous and inspirational. Discovering his family's traumatic experiences and the richness of Estonian culture behind the Iron Curtain offers a compelling and eye-opening read.

ANDRES KASEKAMP

Elmar Tampõld Chair of Estonian Studies,

Professor of History

University of Toronto

Song of my Soul is a powerful memoir centered on the post–World War II Baltic refugee experience, narrated by Dr. Jaak Rakfeldt, who connects the tangible details of history to their psychological impact on his life. Harrowing tales are shared with humanity in a seamless blend of Jaak's story and those of his parents, who witnessed critical moments such as their escape by boat in 1944 and the reestablishment of Estonia's freedom in 1991. Personal turning points carry a lightness and humor, viewed through the lens of years of wisdom. The threads of internal experience intertwine, revealing deeper understandings. This book will resonate with diaspora Estonians everywhere.

MAI-LIIS BARTLING

President, Estonian American National Council

Dr. Jaak Rakfeldt skillfully intertwines his life story as a shy refugee of Estonian heritage who finds himself in the United States with the compelling account of his family's escape from the Soviet invasion of Estonia during World War II. All refugees share the experience of losing their homeland, facing danger while fleeing, and grappling with the challenges of starting anew in an unfamiliar place. However, each story is unique, and Jaak's recounting is a valuable addition to this narrative. He illuminates the struggle of preserving one's cultural heritage while adapting to a new environment. The overview of Estonia and its fate during World War II offers important context for readers who may be unfamiliar with its history.

MARJU RINK-ABEL

Former President, Estonian American National Council

Jaak Rakfeldt's *Song of my Soul* is a beautifully written, profound, and moving memoir that blends personal reflections with family accounts against the broader backdrop of Estonia caught between Hitler and Stalin during World War II. With the insight of a social scientist, Rakfeldt recounts his family's life in Estonia as they endure three successive occupations. He details his family's harrowing escape during Estonia's Mass Flight of 1944—when nearly eighty thousand Estonians fled from Soviet occupation—along with their journey across continents in search of freedom in the U.S. Through historical clarity and moments of vulnerability and humor, he captures not only his family's narrative and his own quest to connect to his culture but also the resilience of an entire generation. At times heartbreaking yet ultimately uplifting, *Song of my Soul* is an engaging, heartfelt read that lingers long after the final page is turned.

LEELO LINASK

Executive Director, Estonian American National Council

Song *of my* Soul

Igaühel on südamelaul, igaühel on see isemoodi.
(Everyone has a unique song in one's soul.)

LEELO TUNGAL, Estonian author and poet

Song *of my* Soul

a memoir

Jaak Rakfeldt

www.mascotbooks.com

Song of My Soul: A Memoir

For more information, please contact:
Mascot Books, an imprint of Amplify Publishing Group
620 Herndon Parkway, Suite 220
Herndon, VA 20170
info@mascotbooks.com

Library of Congress Control Number: 2025907982

CPSIA Code: PRV0825A

ISBN-13: 979-8-89138-712-6

Printed in the United States

I dedicate this book to my parents, Ilmar and Miralda Rakfeldt; my uncle and godfather, Arnold Rakfeldt; and my older sisters, Helle and Tiia. They have all inspired me throughout my life. I have witnessed their capacity to maintain warmth, compassion, kindness, generosity, and a sense of humor, even in the face of the tragedies, dislocations, and all the vicissitudes of our refugee and immigrant experience.

My parents, Ilmar and Miralda Rakfeldt (1997)

Contents

Foreword

Three years after Russia's full-scale invasion of Ukraine on February 24, 2022, Western Europe and the United States have grown impatient and desensitized to the horrors of the Russian occupation. Mass killings have resumed along with deportations, torture, and rape, as well as an influx of refugees to often unwelcoming democracies in the West that inevitably follow a Russian invasion.

The West has seen this before. Unfortunately, it has not learned from it. What it has learned the least is that those who flee—typically targeted for brutal treatment by occupying authorities, including successful farmers, lawyers, doctors, and entrepreneurs—are individuals who enrich the countries they escape to. They enhance those nations culturally, economically, and intellectually, making them better places for everyone to live. These are the stories of success.

Yet, we rarely understand how difficult and challenging it was for those who came to the West—what they and their families endured that ultimately compelled them to flee. People left behind their siblings, parents, and friends. They departed from the places they had always known, taking with them the language and culture in which they had grown up.

Imagine being in that situation: After witnessing shocking and horrific brutality from an invader, you simply pack your belongings and leave for an uncertain future. And when, or rather if, they find a safe place, we seldom hear about the struggles they faced to escape and then establish themselves, often in areas where they were initially unwelcome.

Millions of refugees worldwide, including Jaak Rakfeldt and his family, are scattered. They often face various forms of oppression and exploitation wherever they go. Fortunately, the Rakfeldts found refuge in the welcoming West, specifically in Canada and the United States, where they, like many other refugees, worked hard and achieved success in the land that embraced them.

Professor Rakfeldt's memoir is distinctive because it unveils a nation and culture that many in the West are unaware of. In an era of increasing isolationism and, at times, overt xenophobia, this book examines yet another land that is too often viewed as "a distant place about which we know nothing." This phrase echoes U.K. Foreign Minister Neville Chamberlain's justification in 1938 for conceding to Adolf Hitler's demand to eliminate Czechoslovakia from existence.

The country and culture that captivated Rakfeldt were his own: Estonia, a small nation first occupied by the USSR, then by Nazi Germany, and finally again by the Soviets. This culture was one that both totalitarian regimes sought to suppress, restricting the use of its language and destroying its books and, of course, its literature. It is precisely the poetry of the Estonians that drew

Rakfeldt back to his heritage—a poetry that, like that of other oppressed cultures (for instance, Irish poetry), grapples with existential issues that few in the West have ever faced: the destruction of a millennia-old language, culture, and history. This book illustrates how culture often binds a nation together more than any fleeting media trend.

I hope readers find an aspect of history they know little about in this book, even though it links us to distant people who now live among us.

Toomas Hendrik Ilves is the former president of the Republic of Estonia. He was elected in 2006 and reelected for a second term from 2011 through 2016. President Ilves is credited with making Estonia a world leader in information technology.

Ärma farm
Viljandimaa, Estonia
March 12, 2025

Introduction

This book is a compilation of one Estonian family's experiences as they lived through the tumult and turbulence of the twentieth century during perhaps the most horrific calamity in world history—World War II. It describes the lives of my parents, Ilmar and Miralda Rakfeldt, and their children—Helle, Tiia, and me. My purpose is to enlighten many in the Western world, particularly the younger generations, of the tragic, untold story of the Baltic people through the lens of our family.

Our story parallels those of many others who fled Europe in 1944, who experienced the trauma, coping, and resilience of becoming refugees. They did not want to leave their homes, but they could not stay. (As we say in Estonian, "*Ei tahtnud minna, kuid nad ei saanud jääda.*")

Due to Estonia's strategic geographic location on the eastern shore of the Baltic Sea, foreign invaders have overrun it many times during the last eight hundred years. Through World War II, Estonia suffered brutal invasions and occupations from both the East and the West by Soviet Russia and Nazi Germany. The Yale historian Timothy Snyder describes in heart-wrenching detail the mass murders and atrocities committed during World War II by Hitler and Stalin in territories they controlled following the 1939 Nazi–Soviet Pact. This is the context of my book through the lens of my family's and the Estonian people's experiences (Snyder, T. 2021. *Bloodlands: Europe between Hitler and Stalin*. Basic Books.).

By the war's end, Estonia had lost more than a quarter of its population through mass murders, deportations to remote slave labor camps, and a massive flight to the West.

During the late summer and early fall of 1944, when the Soviets again overran the Baltics, there was a mass exodus of about three hundred thousand people in what came to be called the Great Flight from the three Baltic countries of Estonia, Latvia, and Lithuania. The raging war made escape extremely dangerous. About eighty thousand people fled from Estonia, of whom more than six thousand died or were killed during their flight.

The reason for this escape was the overwhelming fear, fresh in people's memory, of the terror that they had lived through during the first Soviet occupation just three years earlier.

This is my recounting of the story of my journey to discover my heritage, my parents' lives in Estonia from 1918 to the first Soviet Russian occupation, the subsequent Nazi occupation, and their eleventh-hour escape before the onslaught of the second Soviet invasion—the horrific events they endured and the trauma of refugee life. Coping took the form of hard work, flexibility, willingness to do whatever it took to survive, and resilience in the form of solid connections to like-situated others through informal friendship networks and formal associations and organizations. These connections offered emotional and social support, meaning, purpose, and goals, which at their core exemplified the "unwavering, tireless struggle for a free Estonia"—"*Vankumatu, väsimatu võitlus vaba Eesti eest*" (from my September 19, 2022 Estonian Parliament Conference Hall speech).

Over time, once my family arrived in the States, our lives became more comfortable. But for my parents, the deep emotional scars remained. I often heard my father's footsteps in the hallway near my bedroom late at night. Sleeplessness plagued him for years. He never fully recovered from the guilt he felt for surviving while many others perished or were punished severely for their resistance.

My good friend and longtime colleague at the Yale University School of Medicine, Dr. Steven Southwick, studied resilience for years. He listed many of its key components: 1) imitating resilient role models, 2) finding meaning and purpose in trauma, 3) cognitive flexibility, 4) determination and courage, 5) a sense of duty, 6) forgiveness, 7) love, 8) a spiritual practice that strengthens one's moral compass, 9) staying true to one's core values and identity, and 10) solid relationships and social support networks (Southwick, S.M. & Charney, D.S. 2012. *Resilience: The Science of Mastering Life's Greatest Challenges*. Cambridge University Press).

Trauma, coping, and resilience shaped the lives of those who fled in 1944 and have framed the history of our family and thousands of others. Juhan Liiv perhaps foreshadowed this narrative in his poem "*Ta Lendab Mesipuu Poole*" ("He Flies Toward the Beehive [one's homeland]"). Juhan Liiv wrote this poem in 1905 while Estonia was engulfed in the tumult, upheaval, and dislocation of revolution. Later, his words were set to music to become a beautiful, powerful, and emotional staple of the recurring Estonian song festivals. When a chorus of thirty thousand sings before a crowd of thousands, tears flow freely from otherwise emotionally reserved Estonians.

Song has been a significant element of Estonian culture for thousands of years. The first time Estonian words ever appeared in print was in the twelve hundreds: "*Laula! Laula! Pappi!*" ("Sing, sing, priest/father!") (Henry of Livonia. 2003. *The Chronicle of Henry of Livonia*. J. A. Brundage, Trans. Columbia University Press). Choral singing is clearly a way to bolster "solid relationships, social support networks, and identity."

Our parents always yearned for their homeland. I inherited this legacy and try to represent it in these pages.

Ta Lendab Mesipuu Juurde	Flying to Hive and Home
Ta lendab lillest lillesse ja lendab mesipuu poole; ja tõuseb kõuepilv ülesse, ta lendab mesipuu poole. Ja langevad teele tuhanded, veel koju jõuavad tuhanded ja viivad vaeva ja hoole ja lendavad mesipuu poole. Hing, oh hing, sa raskel a'al— kuis õhkad isamaa poole; kas kodu sa, kas võõral maal— kuis ihkad isamaa poole! Ja puhugu vastu sull' surmatuul ja lennaku vastu sull' surmakuul: sa unustad surma ja hoole ning tõttad isamaa poole! Hing, oh hing, sa raskel a'al— kuis õhkad isamaa poole; kas kodu sa, kas võõral maal— kuis ihkad isamaa poole!	Flying from flower to flower, Flying to hive and home; Tho' thunderous clouds may rise, Flying to hive and home. Tho' thousands perish on the way, Still thousands do reach home Along with pain and heed Flying to hive and home. Oh my soul, my burdened soul— Lamenting for my homeland; At home or far abroad— Yearning for my homeland! Whether blasted by deadly winds Or against a deadly salvo: Oblivious both to death and heed Still pressing on to my homeland! Oh my soul, my burdened soul— Lamenting for my homeland; At home or far abroad— Yearning for my homeland!

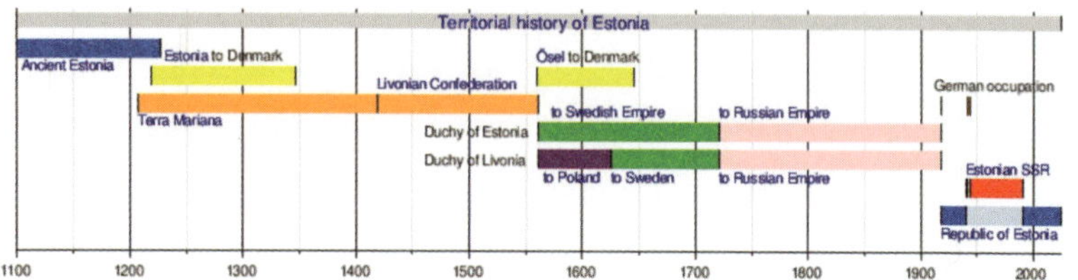

History of Estonia from 1100, showing all of the invasions and occupations.

Location of Estonia. https://www.wikiwand.com/en/articles/History_of_Estonia

Chapter 1

Softly Sung to Self: Song of My Soul

August 1972

My eyes were heavy and drooping shut. I knew it wasn't safe to keep driving. I pulled into a giant shopping plaza parking lot just before the Garden City Skyway that crosses the Welland Canal.

I was driving back from the Forest University Seminar (Metsaülikool in Estonian, or MÜ), the annual summer seminar for youth of Estonian heritage, along the Queen Elizabeth highway at two-thirty in the morning through St. Catharines, Ontario, Canada, in 1972. On my left, I passed the tiny dark-green house my family had lived in when we first immigrated in 1949, while on the right was the schoolhouse my sisters had attended next to Simpson's Garage and Snack Bar where my mother had worked.

I pulled into a far corner of the lot near a light for safety, hoping police wouldn't notice me if overnight parking weren't allowed. I tilted the seat of my Volkswagen Karmann Ghia back as far as it would go and closed my eyes.

As I dozed off, images of the new friends I'd met and our great times during the week in Muskoka filled me with warmth. My struggle to stay awake was the result of long nights by the bonfire playing guitars and singing together.

Singing with Andres was an absolute joy. Andres, a French teacher who had served in the French Foreign Legion, was a popular singer and entertainer who had released many albums of Estonian songs. His voice was a rich, mellow baritone filling the night, accompanied by his guitar, echoing through the forest under the starlit sky, with the warm glow of the fire illuminating his face and his hands embracing his guitar.

I was thrilled that Andres liked and praised my classical guitar style. Accompanied by his deep, full voice, I dared to sing along. With these memories, I drifted off to sleep.

Despite the major trauma of having to flee Europe during and after WWII, most of my parents' generation became strong and healthy middle-class people in their new homes. Hard work brought material well-being and comfort. While they worked hard, they also knew how to enjoy life. Such times were often accompanied by music. They sang, danced, laughed, ate, and often drank until dawn.

A significant factor helping them to cope after the war in their new environments, including the United States where my family wound up, was quickly organizing groups even while still in the European refugee camps. They formed organizations and associations like MÜ where they danced, sang, and made Estonian handicrafts. They also founded congregations, scout troops, Estonian schools, and more. Such organizations fostered a sense of belonging and gave new meaning, goals, and purpose to their lives, all of which strengthened their resilience. Actively participating in these organizations helped them immensely in overcoming their trauma.

When I awoke as the morning sun rose, I grabbed a cup of coffee and a breakfast sandwich at a restaurant in the plaza and headed for the American border. My parents now lived about eighteen miles from the Niagara River, which marks the boundary between the United States and Canada. They were awake when I arrived and were eager to hear how the week had gone. I shared in detail the lectures, the small Estonian language groups, the special interest groups, saunas, and the nights singing songs by the fire. They listened intently. I was thrilled, and perhaps they were astonished, that my Estonian was better than ever. One week of total immersion resurrected the residual language skills I had almost lost.

Sadly, I had to leave early and return to Syracuse because it was Sunday. I worked at Syracuse Psychiatric Hospital and needed to be there first thing Monday morning.

When I arrived at my apartment, I sat down, looked around, and sensed an emptiness and aloneness after so much satisfying, soothing contact with others at MÜ. I had stopped to buy fresh provisions that I used to cook a favorite meal, stir-fried vegetables with thin chicken strips in peanut oil and teriyaki. I ate at my kitchen table using chopsticks, focusing on the food's colors, textures, and aromas in small mouthfuls while listening to Japanese flute music. This dinner with ambient music often grounded and balanced me while fostering greater well-being.

Amid the loneliness, I put my gear from the trip into a closet. I stumbled across a picture I had painted three years earlier on a gray, rainy, lonely Sunday in 1969 when I lived in my college town of Geneseo, New York.

I stared at it for several minutes. Even though the painting was rudimentary and perhaps not very good, it represented my vision of the woman of my dreams.

I placed the painting on a chair across the room where I could see it. A gossamer figure stepped forward from the plain white canvas as though emerging from a reverie. I pulled out my guitar, methodically tuned it, stretched and warmed my fingers by playing scales, and launched into some of my favorite pieces. As typically happened after a while, the music swept me into it, emotionally bringing me to a different place. My sadness lessened.

I was reminded of an Argentinian mythic legend about the origin of the guitar, which tells of a lonely gaucho herding cattle for long periods in the vast emptiness of the pampas. He visits an elderly artisan to tell him of his woes and heartache. The wise elder goes into his workshop and, from his finest woods, fashions a musical instrument with smooth, graceful curves, shaped like a woman, that the gaucho could hold close to him and embrace while making music with the strings to soothe his soul. Sitting in my ragged old chair, I too found solace while embracing my guitar and being comforted with the sound filling my space.

Gazing at my painting, I was struck by how similar the image was to some of the women at the MÜ conference. The thought shot through my mind that having such a woman in my life, with whom I could share our obscure, arcane language, historical roots, cultural traditions, and the anguish of the brutal occupation, could open the door to deepening my connection with the worldwide Estonian diaspora. One immersive week in Muskoka had begun to fill an empty place in my soul.

Songs we had sung around the fire began flowing through my mind. One repeating earworm was about a young man rowing his boat with a young maiden on Lake Viljandi. I hummed the melody; I softly sang to myself the song of my soul.

Viljandi paadimees	Viljandi Boatman
Kui neiu paadis, algab sõit, täis õnne kõik maailm. Ja neiu palgeil punab koit ning rõõmust särab silm. Ah, silmad, need silmad ei iial unune. Need ilusad sinised silmad mul võitsid südame	The maiden's in the boat, the ride begins, the world fills with happiness. The maiden's face reflects the redness of dawn; her eyes are filled with joy. Oh, eyes, those eyes I'll never forget. Those beautiful blue eyes conquered my heart.

Piret played the *kannel*, a traditional Estonian instrument similar to the zither, and I played folk tunes on the guitar before one ardent fan during MÜ.

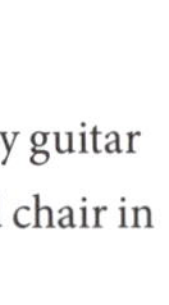

I'm playing my guitar in my tattered chair in Syracuse.

I drove a dove-blue 1968 Volkswagen Karmann Ghia convertible.

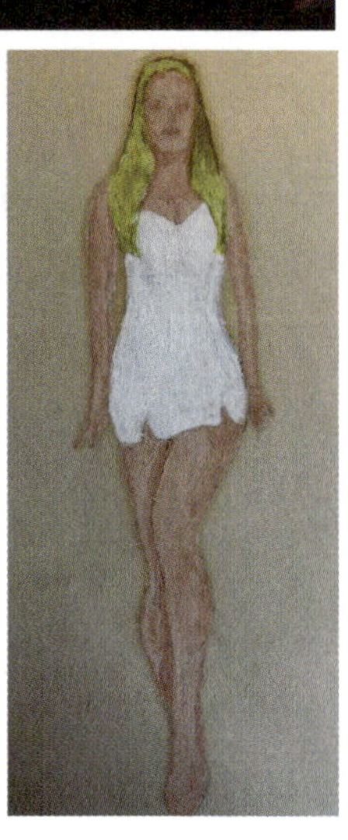

The painting of the woman of my dreams.

Chapter 2

My Dream Woman: A Vision in Gossamer

The early to mid 1970s

My last American girlfriend insightfully confronted me one day while sitting in her living room. She looked into my eyes earnestly and said, "What we have is good, but I always feel that a big door will suddenly slam shut inside you, and I'll be left outside."

Sherry was pretty with dark eyes and hair, petite, passionate, and had been a cheerleader in high school (a boyhood fantasy of mine). We had fun going to clubs with live bands, dancing up a storm, spending time at the beach, and getting together with friends.

One summer in the early 1970s, I stayed with Sherry at her apartment in Syracuse. While with her, I worked on an article manuscript for an Estonian journal. I spent hours in the tiny office in her apartment with English–Estonian dictionaries constantly open. Notes and papers were strewn around the room as I grappled with writing this assignment.

The project was daunting. The writing was slow, word for word, phrase by phrase, and line by line, but I was determined to finish. I markedly improved my Estonian grammar and broadened my vocabulary during this process.

In retrospect, Sherry may have felt abandoned and alone that entire summer. She was left sitting in her living room for long intervals while I worked, cloistered in the small office behind closed doors. When Sherry described her fear of a big door slamming shut in me, it led me to reflect on the relationships I had had going back to the age sixteen.

There was a pattern to my romantic relationships. My first love at age sixteen during my junior year in high school, with Amy, was a deep and powerfully emotional experience. I attended Newfane High while she was at Lockport, a neighboring town. As our relationship intensified, one night in 1963 while walking home along Dale Road from seeing her, it felt like my feet didn't touch the ground. I floated in the air. I thought of her kisses, how she had melted into me, and it was lovely. It was a beautiful time—I was young and in love.

Amy and I attended different colleges in 1964, but somehow, our relationship lasted until the summer after our freshman year. Then, as typically happens with first loves, sadly, ours began to unravel. She wanted to get married at the end of our sophomore year. She planned that she would work while I finished college, and then she would return to finish her degree. But I had done surprisingly well my freshman year; I worried that getting married would jeopardize my ever finishing.

A severe strain emerged, and our relationship continued to unravel. I remember bathing in a tub filled with hot water, trying to feel warm and secure while tears streamed down my face. She later sent me a wallet-sized photo of herself. On the back, she wrote how much being together had meant to her, but she ended with the phrase, "I'm not Estonian."

That summer after freshman year, I kept very busy. I worked briefly at the Harrison radiator factory, where my parents worked, and I worked long hours at a twenty-four-pump cut-rate gas station. This was back when "full service" meant much more than today. I wore a white uniform and washed every customer's front and back window, even if the sale was only one dollar's worth of gasoline, not to mention checking tires and oil when asked. On top of this, my uncle Ottomar hired me to paint their old two-story farmhouse, which entailed much hardscaping before I could paint in the hot sun.

Unexpectedly, while I was painting the house, Amy came to see me. She invited me to a picnic at Krull Park on the shore of nearby Lake Ontario. I was happy to see her but, at the same time, wary of what was to come. For the first time, I felt something tightening, closing off inside of me. The picnic was lovely, albeit awkward. She even sent me a happy birthday telegram before I left for school. Our relationship had ended with ambiguity and confusion, not with a bang but a whimper.

I dated others that summer as well. One stands out: Diana, who had been very popular and active in high school, had been a class leader and on the cheerleading squad. Throughout my school years, I had felt like an outsider, an immigrant kid who didn't belong; she could well have been my dream come true. While our relationship was good, and we had fun—she even came to my fall homecoming weekend sophomore year in college—I felt deadened within and held back emotionally.

Over the next several years, I had other meaningful relationships. In one case, I even lived with a woman for over a year. But, well into our relationship, she pressed me about getting married. Once again, tension, ambivalence, and guilt were evoked in me.

My sister Helle, a college art professor and artist, had given me painting supplies for a birthday, which were promptly neglected. In late 1969, while living in Genesco, my college town, I felt the need to translate my feelings into something more concrete by painting my vision of the perfect woman. I had lived with this image in my head for a long time; I aimed to convey it onto canvas. Sitting alone in my apartment on a cold, rainy, gray Sunday afternoon, I vowed to realize my vision, hoping to ease my loneliness.

I pulled the paints from the bottom of a drawer where they had been left unused and stared at the blank canvas for a long time. Never having studied painting, I was intimidated by the task. Finally, after focusing on it and imagining how it could appear, I began using mechanical drawing skills I'd learned in high school. I laid out the proportions of the painting, measuring precisely and marking the canvas with faint pencil marks, careful not to have them noticeably visible through the paint.

After tentatively, anxiously outlining a female figure, placing dots and short dashes, I dipped my #1 brush into the oil paint and began carefully applying it. I worked very slowly and methodically, spending hours on this task. It was late into the night before I finished. I wondered whether I should create a setting to surround her. After pondering this, I left her stepping forward from the blank white canvas, a gossamer, dreamlike woman.

This image always stayed with me on some level. Perhaps Sherry had intuitively sensed this through her metaphor of the "big door slamming shut."

Chapter 3

Family Roots

The love of Estonia runs deep in my family.

My earliest known Estonian family dates from the 1700s. My mother was born in Vedra Küla, in Läänemaa, close to Haapsalu on the west coast. On my mother's side, I trace my family back to my great, great, great, great, great, great grandfather. Like most Estonians at the time, the patriarch in my mother's family tree did not have a family name but was known merely as Pawel from Saunja, born circa 1700.

The tiny village of Saunja (even today, only about 110 residents) is on Saunja Bay, which empties into the Baltic Sea, and is very near Räägu Mõis (Räägu Manor), where my parents lived. Pawel's son was Saunja Pawli Hans, born circa 1720. Han's son, Mango Ado Jüri, was born in 1766. Veski Ott Laanberg/Metsberg was born in 1783, and his wife Liisu was the daughter of Mango Ado Jüri. They were the parents of my great-grandfather Jüri Laanberg (born in 1843). His son Jaan Laanberg was born in 1886. He changed his family name to Laanepere in 1936. He was my mother's father and my grandfather.

On my father's side, I can trace my family back to my great-grandfather, Juhan Rakvelt or Rakwald. With his first wife, perhaps named Kröõt, he had two sons Juhan Rakvelt (Rakwald), born in 1853, and Jakob, born in 1852. After his first wife died, Juhan married Marie Kassik, who gave birth to my grandfather Kustav Rakvelt.

Great-grandfather Juhan divided the original farm, Mardi Talu, into three equal parts for his sons. Dividing the farmland, the pastureland, and the forest into three equal parts resulted in a patchwork of pieces for each son. My father, Ilmar Rakvelt, was born to Kustav Rakvelt (1873–1953) and Marie Rakvelt (Silm) (1877–1921) on Kustav's parcel of land, known as Oja Talu (River Farm). It was named as such because the Ambla River flows through the property. It also flows through Ambla, the nearby village in Järvamaa. Parts of Oja farm were on each side of the river, often flooding in the spring.

My father was born in 1915 on May 29 (according to the Julian calendar) or June 11 (in the Gregorian calendar). We always celebrated his birthday on June 11. The family name was changed to Rakfeldt at some point during the first years of my father's life.

After independence in 1918, many people also changed their names to sound more Estonian. Thus, the family name Laanberg became Laanepere. During serfdom, people were known by the names of their manors, followed by their first names. Interestingly, to this day, it is common for people to be referred to not by their first and last names, which is the custom in the United States, but rather by the name of their locale, farm, or village, followed by their first names. It would be like saying, "Newfane Jaak." All the farms have names identifying people; for example, my mother would have been referred to as Aru Miralda, my aunt Tamme Ida, and my father Oja Ilmar.

To go back even further, the first homo sapiens settled in Estonia after the glaciers had receded around 8,500 BCE. Proto-Finno-Ugrians inhabited the Estonian area and spoke Uralic. This language is a member of the Finnic branch, closely related to Finnish. It is unrelated to the languages of its bordering countries, Russian and Latvian, which are both Indo-European.

Ancient Estonians had a highly developed social structure with elected leaders. They were pantheistic, believing that all living things possessed a spirit. They worshipped the spirits of nature in unique and sacred places within the forests. They believed that the souls of their ancestors resided in the saunas.

During the Viking period, Estonia was subject to raids. Estonians, particularly from the big island of Saaremaa, also plundered and pillaged Swedish settlements along the Baltic coast. On a more peaceful note, Estonia's geographic location lent itself to active trading between the East and West during this period.

Starting with the Northern Crusades, Estonia became a battleground for centuries. Denmark, Germany, Russia, Sweden, and Poland fought many wars over controlling Estonia due to its crucial geographical position as a gateway between East and West. Estonian freedom ended with the attacks and invasion by the Germanic Christian crusaders throughout the early thirteenth century. The Baltic Sea land along Estonia's eastern coast was the last part of Europe to be Christianized. In 1193, Pope Celestine called for a crusade against the pagans of the north and declared this area to be called Terra Mariana or the "Land of Mary." Although to this day Estonians sometimes refer to their homeland as "Marjamaa" ("the Virgin Mary's land"), many Estonians view this violent and forced Christianization as a tragic loss of their freedom to foreign occupiers and the beginning of seven hundred years of domination, exploitation, and servitude.

After Danes and Germans conquered the area in 1227, Estonia was initially ruled in the north by Denmark's Livonian Order, an autonomous part of the Monastic State of the Teutonic Knights and the Baltic German ecclesiastical states of the Holy Roman Empire. From 1418 to 1562, Estonia formed part of the Livonian Confederation. After the Livonian War of 1558–1583, Estonia became part of the Swedish Empire until 1710, when Sweden ceded it to Russia following the Great Northern War. It was at the Treaty of Nystad in 1721 that Sweden formally surrendered the area to the Russians. Czar Peter the Great's field marshal, Boris Sheremetev, wrote proudly to Peter in 1709 that no longer did a cock crow or a dog bark from Lake Peipsi on the Eastern border of Estonia to the Gulf of Riga on the Western frontier; such was the extent of the destruction. Only about one hundred thousand Estonians survived in 1720. They were victims of both a plague and war. The population of the capital, Tallinn, dropped from about ten thousand to two thousand people.

Estonia then became a part of the Russian Empire until 1918. The Baltic-German nobility enjoyed autonomy throughout this period, and German served as the language of administration and education. At the same time, the Estonians were the serfs who worked the land and belonged to the manors of the German nobility. Our family name (Rakwald, Rakvelt, Rakfeldt) may have originated from my ancestors having lived and worked as serfs on the nearby Raka Mõis (Raka Manor) near the town of Ambla, where their homes were at the time of my father's birth.

The Enlightenment (1750–1840) helped lead to an Estonian national awakening that developed momentum in the later 1800s. It began with the historic song festival of 1869, officially branded as a festival celebrating the fiftieth anniversary of the 1819 end of serfdom in Estonia. Records exist of the last Estonian serfs being sold on the block in 1789. The price for a single man was thirty to forty rubles; for a girl, it was ten rubles, and for a child, it was four rubles. A whole family could be purchased for one hundred rubles. Simultaneously there was a heavy-handed attempt to Russify the Estonian population throughout the last half of the nineteenth century and stretching into the beginning of the twentieth. It finally ended with the Estonian War of Independence.

In the aftermath of World War I (1914–1918) and the Russian Revolution of 1917, Estonians declared independence on February 24, 1918. After this, the Estonian War of Independence from 1918 to 1920 ensued on two fronts. The newly proclaimed state fought against Bolshevist Russia to the east and against the Baltic German forces of the Baltische Landeswehr to the south. The Tartu Peace Treaty, signed on February 2, 1920, marked the end of the fighting. With it, Russians recognized Estonian independence "in perpetuity."

During the years of independence, Estonia was proud of its treatment of its minorities. A clear example of the tolerance and benevolence of Estonians toward ethnic minorities is reflected in the Law of Cultural Self-Government for the National Minorities, enacted on February 12, 1925. This law gave minority groups autonomy in educational and cultural fields. It provided state-supported institutions for developing each minority group's language and culture. The cultural autonomy legislation gave these rights to the Baltic-German, Russian, and Swedish people in Estonia, along with its tiny Jewish community (listed as having only 3,045 people). To commemorate the tenth anniversary of this declaration of Estonian independence in 1918, a document was published in 1928 in both Hebrew and Yiddish confirming the rights of the Jewish community to full autonomy. This document is now housed in the Jewish National Library in Jerusalem.

In addition, in 1928, Tartu University established a chair in Jewish studies, which was unique in Eastern Europe, strongly supported by Albert Einstein. Lord Acton once noted that since "its respect for minorities best measures the civilization of a state," Estonia was therefore highly civilized.

Things took a horrible turn in 1940 in the wake of the Nazi–Soviet Pact, known as the Molotov–Ribbentrop Treaty, signed on August 23, 1939. This treaty created an allyship between the USSR and Germany prior to the outbreak of World War II. The Soviet Union took this opportunity to occupy Estonia in 1940. The United States, with the Welles Declaration issued on July 23, 1940 by Sumner Welles, the acting U.S. Secretary of State, condemned the June 1940 occupation by the Soviet army of the three Baltic countries—Estonia, Latvia, and Lithuania—and refused to recognize their subsequent annexation diplomatically. The European Court of Human Rights declared this Soviet act an illegal annexation of the country, but nothing more was done to stop it.

The first Soviet occupation only lasted a year. In 1941, during Operation Barbarossa, Nazi Germany betrayed Russia and ousted the Soviets from occupied Estonia. At first, the Estonian people hailed the Nazi "liberation" from the Soviet terror they had endured, but the Nazi occupation was no better. It resulted in more executions, appropriations, conscription into the German army, and a lack of independence.

Three years later, as Germany crumbled under the Allied assault, the Soviet Union again occupied Estonia in September 1944. This led to fifty years of brutal occupation and annexation. My personal and familial story unfolded during the decades of this occupation.

Laul Põhjamaast	Song of the Northland
Põhjamaa, me sünnimaa, tuulte ja tuisuööde maa, range maa ja kange maa, virmaliste maa.	Land of the North, land of our birth, Land of winds and blustery nights, Land of harshness, land of vigor, Land of northern lights.
Põhjamaa, me sünnimaa, iidsete kuuselaante maa, lainte maa ja ranna maa, sind ei jäta ma.	Land of the North, land of our birth, Land of forests ages-old, Land of tides, land lined by shores, Forsake you I never can.
On lumme uppund metsasalud, vaiksed taliteed, nii hellad on su aisakellad, lumel laulvad need.	Snow covered forest groves, Silent winter paths, Sleighbells softly Ringing on the snow.
Põhjamaa, me sünnimaa, karmide meeste kallis maa, taplemiste tallermaa, püha kodumaa.	Land of the North, land of our birth, Land by rugged men cherished, Land by battles trodden, My home and sacred land.
Põhjamaa, me sünnimaa, hinges sind ikka kannan ma, kaugeil teil sa kallis meil, sind ei jäta ma.	Land of the North, land of our birth, Held forever in my soul, In far off lands, cherished still, Forsake you I never will.

My mother's parents: Jaan and Anna Laanepere.

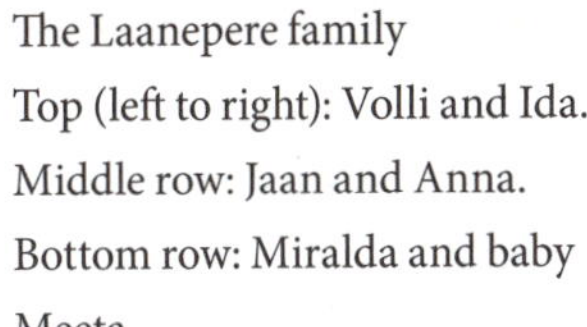

The Laanepere family
Top (left to right): Volli and Ida.
Middle row: Jaan and Anna.
Bottom row: Miralda and baby Meeta.

My mother's childhood home, Aru Talu.

My father's childhood home, Oja Tau. I'm standing with my cousin Kalju Nugis.

Oja farm was divided by the Ambla River, which often flooded during the spring.

The flooded Ambla River (#1 Arnold; #3 Father's cousin August; #2 Ottomar).

The Laaepere family.

Left to right: my mother, Bernhard, Meeta.

Chapter 4

From Refuge to Restlessness: Navigating New Worlds

Late 1940s

I was born in an Estonian refugee enclave in Sweden in 1946, right after the Second World War. My early years were filled with tales of atrocities and stories of loss and longing. I vividly remember as a little boy stretching tall to stare over the stone windowsill of our Stockholm apartment, imagining that I saw Russians outside coming to attack us. As young as I was, I drew maps showing how I would lead the fight to liberate my homeland.

Our apartment building was filled with Estonian refugees. It was a kid's paradise. Playing with so many other children filled my days with fun and frolic. I felt safe in our tight-knit community despite the dark times my parents had endured. They did their best to make our lives sunny and bright.

I had many young friends with whom to play and romp around. Our apartment building was surrounded by tall, old pine trees with big outcroppings of rocks sprinkled between them. One bright, sunny summer day, we played king of the castle, running from boulder to boulder, scrambling to be the first to the top. We'd jump off and run to the next.

As I climbed up a big boulder where my friend Rita sat at the top, she yelled, "Kaagu's here." As a three-year-old, she twisted up the sounds of my name, Jaak. She repeated "Kaagu's climbing up" in a playful, affectionate, fun tone. Soon, the other kids, my sisters, parents, and close family friends called me Kaagu too. During adulthood, my sisters stopped using it so much, but my parents continued fondly calling me Jaak or Kaagu.

A major crisis came when my sister Helle, then eight years old, was sent to a tuberculosis sanitorium for several months. Three-year-old me missed her so much. When she returned by train along with a nurse and several other kids, we met her at the Stockholm Central Train Station. Engulfed by the noise, steam, clatter, and crowds, I saw her come from behind as she got off the train, and I ran up, slipping my little hand into hers. I was so happy, I cried. She did too as she turned and hugged me. Now Helle (born 1941), Tiia (born 1942), and I were together again.

Sadly, for my parents, the dark cloud of Stalin's terror continued to hang over us and our community, even after they'd fled Estonia. Moscow constantly pressured the leftist Swedish government to send Baltic refugees back. At the time, the only Western nation that recognized the Russian illegal occupation and annexation of Estonia as legitimate was Sweden. Horrifically, some people, mostly Latvians, were being deported. I've seen news photos of men cutting their wrists as they were led out toward the dock to the waiting ship. Some Estonian refugees in Sweden pooled their money and bought old sailboats and fishing boats that they fixed up and secretly set off for America. Men, women, children, and whole families desperately sailed across the treacherous North Atlantic for several weeks to reach America.

My *ema*, the Estonian word for mother, received letters from the Soviet embassy in Stockholm urging her to return to Estonia by describing how happy people were, how good life was, and how her family missed her so much. She and my father, or *isa*, did not believe it. The truth was that terror reigned back home with random arrests of innocent people, who would disappear, never to be seen again. Just as frightening, receiving those letters from the Russians at our Stockholm apartment meant the KGB knew exactly where we lived.

Immediately upon coming to Sweden in 1944, my parents applied to immigrate to the United States. The yearly quota for Estonians was tiny, leading to uncertainty about when it would ever happen. In contrast, Canada was immediately accepting people. So, my parents decided we should go to Canada in the fall of 1949.

Our trip from Southampton, U.K., to Halifax, N.S., Canada, when I was three years old is a vivid memory. We spent a week rocked by the stormy North Atlantic; everyone was sick, and the staff didn't pay much attention to us. Instead, they pulled down the ornate woodwork of the floating palace, the *Aquitania*, and cut up the dark red curtains as souvenirs. This was the last voyage of the famous ship before it would be turned into scrap metal.

The smell of the ship was unmistakable in my olfactory memory. Later, when we visited Niagara Falls in Canada, the disinfectant aroma of the public bathrooms reminded me of our ship. The constant swaying made people sick—like nothing my little body had ever known.

To our surprise and dismay, Canadian customs officials wouldn't allow us to leave Halifax Harbor. My *onu* (uncle), who lived across the border in the United States, was not allowed to be our Canadian sponsor. They locked us in Pier 21, men in one hall and women and children in another.

We managed to get out and board a train. Our train arrived in St. Catharines, Ontario, twenty-four hours late. Onu Ottomar had come over the border to Canada to meet us and take us to our new home.

We moved into a tiny green three-room house that Onu had arranged for us to rent on the farm of the Joll family. The Jolls had come from Estonia before the war and had just built a new house next to our little green one.

St. Catharines is called the Garden City. Fruit orchards and vineyards surrounded us. I remember when we arrived, there was fresh fallen snow and the sweet scent of smoke from the apple and cherry wood burned to heat homes.

The Joll children were Ines, Peeter, and Rita, all older than me. I felt isolated and mostly spent time with my sisters. But the older children immediately started going to the school across the QEW.

Canada was so different from Sweden, where I always had other kids to play and have fun with. Now, I spent much time wandering around our yard, the barn, and the chicken house, mostly alone.

When our family finally got permission to immigrate to the United States, we stayed for a few weeks at Onu Ottomar's house in Niagara County, a fruit-growing region on the shore of Lake Ontario.

It was tight accommodations, with ten people living in a small two-bedroom farmhouse. The older kids, Tiia and Helle and our cousins Harry and Johnnie, slept in a tent pitched in the yard when the weather was dry and before it got cold. It was a relief when we moved into our nearby rented tenant house on Mr. Herr's big fruit farm. I recall when Ottomar and my father set up the black chimney pipe for the potbelly stove during our first night in the new place. I warmed myself by backing up close to it.

I liked hanging out with my cousins and I looked up to Harry and Johnnie and had fun with them, but it still wasn't the same as Sweden. I was sad. I lost my appetite. Food didn't smell or taste good anymore, which created conflict at home. My parents always insisted that we clean our plates completely. They taught us it was a sin to waste food. For centuries, Estonian peasants lived on the edge of famine and starvation, depending on how the harvest had been from year to year. I had been a chubby kid in Sweden and happy with all my friends. In America, I became thinner, quieter, and somewhat withdrawn. Mealtimes were times of tension.

One evening, I sat poking at my half-eaten potatoes, meatloaf with brown gravy, and carrots. I refused to finish the food on my plate. My parents yelled at me to clean my plate. Suddenly, my father rose from his chair. I froze. He dragged me toward the door, opened it, and pushed me into the cold, dark woodshed.

As I stood alone in the dark woodshed, tears flowed down my face. Then, I heard Muri, our curly-furred, floppy-eared, big black cocker spaniel, climbing the rickety stairs into the shed. He nudged me with his wet nose and licked my hands, wrists, and arms. I looked down into his big brown eyes. Stroking his head and scratching behind his ears, I leaned forward and whispered, "Muri, *mu sober.*" ("Muri, you're my friend."). I don't recall how that night ended; I only remember the comfort of my furry friend.

Once I was in school, I recall riding home in the yellow school bus that squeaked and bumped to each stop. The bus dropped me off in front of our weathered, dark-gray, unpainted, shingled tenant house. There was no indoor plumbing and no central heat. An outhouse stood behind the leaning garage. There was a low-roofed red chicken coop and a corrugated metal pigsty. Other kids had returned to their big white houses with lush green lawns and manicured shrubs. I wondered, what would it have been like to live in a place like that—to live more like they did?

I wasn't happy in America. At home, we spoke Estonian, but in school, everyone spoke English. I felt out of place. I did not belong. Kids made fun of me one day on the school bus because I wore short pants like young boys in Sweden. But here, no one wore shorts to school during cold weather.

A refugee and an immigrant kid who barely spoke English, I started school at Newfane Central School in Newfane, New York, Niagara County. On the first day of class, while calling the roll, the teacher said, "Jack." No one responded. She repeated it, but there was still no response. Kids began looking around. I wondered, did she mean me? Finally, I slowly offered, "My name is Jaak."

She leaned forward toward me, pointed her finger, and said sternly, "In America, you are Jack." She was big. I was little. Others laughed. It appeared I was too stupid to even know my own name, so I capitulated and became "Jack" until I left Newfane.

I felt estranged, alone, wounded, as though a piece of me had been torn away. Only after college did I finally take back my real name. All along, I had lived in two different identity worlds. For my family and Estonians, I was Jaak, while in my American world, I had become Jack.

This episode and other painful experiences during my early school years made me feel like an outsider, which fostered insecurity, shyness, awkwardness, and resentment. I never told anyone about these feelings. Nobody ever knew. Instead, my external school years were relatively normal. I had friends, played sports, attended school activities, dances, proms, and had fun. I could hide my loneliness well.

As a youngster, I was always shy and quiet. I needed more confidence, especially around young women. This changed dramatically during a trip to Canada's Crystal Beach amusement park. My budding friendship with Amy, mentioned before as my first love, flowered during the Laff-in-the-Dark amusement ride. We sat in a tiny car moving along a track inside a dark building. In pitch-black darkness, we were pulled along in our tiny car past various scary images with frightening, spine-chilling sounds. The car creaked, bumped, and made sharp, unexpected turns, jostling and bouncing us against each other in the sheer darkness.

Our faces brushed against each other. Our cheeks touched. I turned my face toward her. My arm that had been around her shoulder gently pulled her toward me. Our lips touched. Moving against me, she eagerly and gently pushed her lips against mine.

Surges of sheer bliss shot through me. I didn't want this moment to end. But, much too soon, our car lurched and jolted out into the bright sunlight. I trembled as I climbed out of the car. I stumbled as we walked away from the Laff-in-the-Dark ride. The world was no longer as it had been.

As mentioned, our relationship eventually ended during college. The words on that photo Amy sent me at the end stayed in my mind: "But I am not Estonian." Amy's words portended something significant.

My first day of school was in 1951, with Helle, Tiia, and my cousins Johnnie and Maire, and my second cousin Kathy.

St. Catharines: Isa, Florence, Ema, Ottomar (1949).

My cousins Harry, Helle, and Tiia. Johnnie, me (with the hat from Sweden), cousin Marie (1949).

Chapter 5

Sweet Salty Bitterness

Christmas 1969

On Christmas Day 1969, when I was twenty-three years old, a huge nor'easter swept up the East Coast, dumping over forty inches of snow in central and northern New York and Vermont. The full brunt, which took more than twenty lives as it swept through the northeast from the south into New England and Quebec, spared us at my parents' place in Newfane, north of Buffalo. We got some snow and wind, but not the worst of it.

The soothing warmth of the woodstove made the kitchen even cozier. As a child, I would run downstairs from our unheated second floor and push my back up to the stove. My mother often made Swedish-style pancakes, thin like crepes. I would cover them with jam and maple syrup and eat them with salty sausage links. My palate savored the contrasting mingling of sweet and salt.

After our usual Christmas Eve church, gift-giving, and traditional Christmas dinner, I spent that holiday with my sisters and their children before they left. Now, I was alone with my parents, enjoying our conversation, the stove's warmth, the pancakes. This was the best time to discuss something I had been reluctant to bring up. Much like the sweet pancakes, seeing Estonia, the country of my origin, was a delicious fantasy I harbored.

For a long time, I had wanted to visit the homeland my parents had escaped from in 1944. I knew they disapproved of this idea, and it wasn't only them. Within the entire exile community, it was strongly discouraged to visit Soviet-occupied Estonia. Going there would legitimize the illegal occupation and annexation by having to apply to them for a visa.

And I still remembered vividly March 5, 1953, when we heard on the radio that Joseph Stalin had died. My mother curled up in the corner of the couch, sobbing uncontrollably. Such an outpouring of emotion on the part of either of my parents was extremely rare, almost nonexistent, but the pain that madman and butcher of innocent people had caused her, our family, and millions of others was too much for her to bear.

I was afraid to mention the possibility of going to Estonia because I knew it would trouble my parents. But we had also heard about the Centennial Song Festival earlier that year, which marked the one hundredth anniversary of the first song festival at the University City of Tartu in 1869.

As mentioned earlier, the 1869 Song Festival had been officially billed as marking fifty years from the end of serfdom in Estonia in 1819. In addition to patriotic songs, the festival featured powerful nationalist speeches from scholars and leaders of the National Awakening movement. This National Awakening era continued through the second half of the nineteenth century into the early twentieth.

While the abolition of serfdom in 1819 was a significant step toward legal freedom for Estonian peasants, it did not immediately lead to economic independence or social equality. The effects of this reform were complex and laid the groundwork for future struggles and changes in Estonian society, such as the rise of a national consciousness and identity and the striving for independence.

But the end of serfdom was still significant even though Estonian peasants continued to live hard lives. They still had to rent land from their landlords and share their produce as payment, leaving them struggling for subsistence during bad growing seasons. The important thing is that with the end of serfdom, Estonian peasants gained greater freedom. They were allowed to own property and land and adopt surnames.

This too was a period of intense Russification of Estonia, so in order to get permission to hold a festival with patriotic songs and speeches, organizers characterized it as the fiftieth anniversary of the end of serfdom in 1819. And so, fifty years later in 1869, the first song festival marked this important anniversary.

The festivals continued every five or so years even through the fifty years of Soviet occupation. The Russians, of course, used these events to promote their ideology and propaganda, demanding there be far less Estonian content in the program. The Soviets used the song festivals to enforce Russification, insisting that only Soviet songs praising the Revolution and Communism be sung. Nevertheless, Estonians turned out for these events in order to collectively experience at least a brief interval of national unity and identity with the iconic, traditional Estonian songs that were left.

For the most part, the Estonian people went along with Russian interference to avoid trouble. In 1969, the hundred-year anniversary of the first song festival, things went differently.

Estonians anticipated a large celebration, so the Soviet authorities sought to squelch the Estonian spirit. They discouraged wearing traditional Estonian folk costumes and forbade the singing of "*Mu Isamaa on Minu Arm*," the unofficial national anthem.

But that summer, the choir refused to leave the stage as the crowd shouted to sing the song. They started to sing the anthem without a leader, not one, not two, not three times—repeatedly. The Soviets were forced to let the composer, Gustav Ernesaks, take the stage and conduct the song. After the festival, Russians threatened to ban the singing of "*Mu Isamaa on Minu Arm*" from the festival program in the future.

Although 1970 would not be a song festival year, I wanted to see Estonia for myself. Now, that Christmas of 1969 with my parents, I debated bringing up the idea of my traveling there. I knew it would take months to get a visa through the Soviet bureaucracy in Moscow. If I wanted to go in the summer when the weather was warm and the days were long with the midnight sun, I had to start the process in January.

I stared out the window at the freshly fallen snow for a while. After gathering my courage, I turned and said, "*Tahan sel suvel Eestit külastada.*" ("I want to visit Estonia this summer.")

Isa stared out the window and sat motionless. Ema stared at the ceiling with an ashen, aghast expression. My parents rarely expressed their emotions. I never heard them argue or fight. Our culture is one where feelings are muted and restrained. My words had opened old wounds, but I couldn't unsay what I had said.

After a long silence, Isa turned, looked at me intensely with deep brown eyes, and implored, "*Palun ära mine.*" ("Please don't go.") Still, with a shocked look, Ema agreed, nodding slowly. "It's too dangerous for our family who is still there," Isa continued. "Our family has suffered so much. Contact with the West may mean trouble. It may mean losing their jobs. And, if they're out of work, they may also lose their apartments, which are allocated through peoples' jobs. It is a crime to be unemployed there. The KGB could interrogate them. They could face made-up charges about helping the United States. Our relatives could be arrested and jailed."

I stared at the floor. Although he was speaking calmly, this was tantamount to a despairing outburst. Their reaction was far worse than I had feared it would be.

We sat at the round oak kitchen table set in the bay window of the kitchen. It overlooked a huge old maple tree and a pasture covered with freshly fallen snow gleaming in the bright sunlight. The claw-footed table had been there for years. Leaning against it gave me a feeling of security and stability. As a family, we enjoyed meals together and talking around it. But now I felt remorse about having brought back painful memories.

I said, "I could go only with an Intourist group and have no contact with family." Intourist was the only officially sanctioned way to travel in the Soviet bloc, and it included constant monitoring and surveillance.

Isa still shook his head no. "Your Rakfeldt name alone will cause trouble." Isa reminded me about Ago Talvar, who escaped to Sweden with us on the same boat in 1944. He and Isa had created the Western Estonian self-defense unit and fought battles together against the Russians. They pushed out the retreating Russians toward the East as the Germans invaded from the West. "The Soviets haven't forgotten. Only about five years ago, they held a show trial where they sentenced Ago to death in absentia." He looked downward again.

In their retreat, Stalin had declared a "scorched earth" program, during which death squads roamed the countryside, killing, raping, burning, and destroying everything as they withdrew. The self-defense units protected innocent Estonian civilians from their marauding destruction. Moreover, rather than being arrested, my parents fled into the woods in 1941 and joined a group of armed partisans.

Isa told me about how he lived with the pain and guilt of having hidden arms inside the foundation stones of the barn at Ema's home, Aru Talu. The Russians arrested Ema's parents and her younger brother Bernhard, whom they brutally tortured. Finally, Bernhard broke and told them about the stash of weapons. While Isa told me this story, tears streamed down Ema's cheeks.

I leaned forward, head bowed, and said, "*Eestisse ma ei lähe.*" ("I won't go to Estonia.") Not that year, anyway. I felt sick. I hurt from having caused Isa and Ema such anguish.

Only minutes earlier, we had been enjoying the kitchen's woodstove's coziness. The aroma of Ema's pancakes and the delicious sweetness of jam and maple syrup were like my delicious fantasy of seeing our homeland. But how I had reminded my parents of their painful past left a bitter salty sausage aftertaste.

Majakene Mere Ääres	A House by the Sea
Kui on meri hülgehall ja sind ründamas suur hall. Kui on meri hülgehall ja sind ründamas on suur hall. Nõnda hea on mõelda siis, et kuskil rannaliiv ja mere ääres väike maja ootamas on mind. Refr.: Nii hea, nii hea on mõelda siis, et kuskil rannaliiv ja mere ääres väike maja ootamas on mind. Seal, kus vana kaev on, kriiksuv aiavärav on. Seal, kus vana kaev on, kriiksuv aiavärav, värav on. Akna taga õhtu eel, vaatad mere poole veel. Ja mere ääres väike maja ootamas on mind.	When the sea is seal gray and a large gray wave attacks you. When the sea is seal gray and there's a big gray wave attacking you. It's so good to think then, that somewhere on the beach sand a small house stands by the sea and is waiting for me. Refrain: So good, so good is to think then that somewhere on the beach sand a small house stands by the sea and is waiting for me. Where the old well stands, the garden gate creaks. Where the old well stands, the garden gate creaks. By the window in early evening, you still look out toward the sea. In the small house by the sea that waits for me.

Chapter 6

From Awkwardness to Belonging, Confidence, and Community

Summer 1972

So, due to my parents' reaction to my plans of traveling to Estonia, I determined to get as close as possible to my Estonian heritage in other ways. Getting involved with MÜ played an essential role in finding, maintaining, and strengthening my Estonian identity. It radically changed my life.

I had lived removed from the Estonian community for many years before I went to MÜ for the first time in 1972. I had never attended an Estonian Saturday School or belonged to other Estonian youth groups. After I left for college at age seventeen, I didn't have the opportunity to speak much Estonian for years, leading to a loss of fluency and confidence.

In my twenties, I had heard that MÜ was where young, educated, and creative Estonians gathered for one week each summer in a remote area of the Muskoka Lakes region of Ontario, Canada, about one hundred miles north of Toronto. My parents helped me fill out the application in Estonian and write an essay about my interest in attending.

I anxiously waited. Then the good news came! I was accepted. But the bad news was I became overwhelmed with anxiety about what I had gotten myself into. I knew no one who would be attending. I am, by nature, quiet and shy. MÜ would be a week-long Estonian language immersion. I had little confidence in my Estonian language skills. Despite all this, I felt this was where I needed to go. And so, I cast fate to the wind that July and embarked on the seven-hour journey from Syracuse, New York, to the Muskoka Lakes Region of Ontario in my VW Karmann Ghia convertible.

The sun was warm, and the wind blew against my face and through my hair, refreshing me. I felt the freedom and joy of the open road. But inevitably, the dreaded anticipation and anxiety of what lay ahead returned. It took the form of imagining being out of place and alone for a whole week among Estonian speakers in a remote wooded location.

My anxiety stemmed from my lack of confidence in speaking this complex language, with its intricate grammar and phonetics. My pronunciation was perfect from speaking it with my family until starting school when we arrived in America, but little else remained. Nevertheless, on some level, my decision to undertake this journey was an effort to connect with something to fill the emptiness deep within me. I needed to connect with my heritage despite the uncertainties and language barriers that lay ahead. This trip was a testament to my determination to bond once more with my Estonian identity, to fill the hole in my spirit I had lived with for so long.

On the first evening, the legendary Professor Ivar Ivast gave a witty and poetic talk. He ended with the following lines:

"*Metsaülikoolis abielluvad kivid ja puud, südamed ja pead . . . kodu ja maa, maa ja ilm, kodumaa ja maailm.*" ("Forest University weds together, stones and trees, hearts and minds—home and land, homeland and world.")

My heart leaped that I was fully understanding not only the language of Ivast's eloquent words but also their meaning. I was blessed to be there.

After Ivast finished, as an icebreaker, Vello Sermat, a psychologist, directed each of us to talk to someone we didn't know. I tried to hide behind a narrow post in the hall's center. I was stunned when Ivast walked over to me and asked who I was and why I had come.

I stared at him with a wide-open mouth and couldn't say anything. After an awkward silence, I mumbled my name and added that I enjoyed his talk. I wanted to sink under the floor and sneak away.

I then slinked along the wall toward the side door and went outside. I returned to my tiny seven-by-seven-foot tent, which was too low to stand in. I sat in the middle of it cross-legged, wrestling with what I should do next. I thought of quietly packing my car and secretly driving off into the night toward home.

Indulging in this reverie momentarily relieved my anguish. But after a few moments, I realized that leaving would worsen things. A crisis would be declared; a manhunt would be organized. Police would be called. They'd think I was lost in the woods or drowned in the lake. My shame would become magnified into a public crisis; perhaps in the local media, it would read: AMERICAN LOST NEAR KOTKAJÄRVE SCOUT CAMP. (I have nothing if not a vivid imagination.)

I chose instead to slowly climb back up the hill toward the main hall. I slid stealthily into the hall through a side door. People were mingling, drinking wine, and having hors d'oeuvres. I grabbed a glass and an open-faced smoked salmon sandwich. I slowly moved around among the people.

A lovely young woman named Inga approached me. We made small talk in Estonian, learning that we had both lived in St. Catharines, Ontario. As we talked, my anxiety lessened. I let myself flow into the discussion without judging myself or my language skills. I began meeting interesting, creative, warm, and wonderful people.

In addition to the lectures, we had small group discussions, concerts, folk dancing, sauna nights, swimming, and singing together deep into the night around bonfires. Something inside me felt nourished and fulfilled, and the week ended with a real old-fashioned Estonian wedding and a celebration of the marriage filled with great food and drink, music, dancing, and singing. My week in Muskoka saved me from merely melting into the American mainstream society. I had finally touched who I am in the recesses of myself. After such an inauspicious beginning, I ended up presenting lectures and workshops at MÜ over the years and even receiving an honorary doctorate in 1994. In 2022, attesting to my language skills, I presented a speech in Estonian at the Estonian Parliament Conference Hall, urging Parliament to designate a day of remembrance for those who fled in 1944.

Receiving an honorary doctorate at Metsaülkool (1994).

Presenting a lecture at MÜ (1991).

Chapter 7

From War-Torn Youth and Grief to Western Estonia: My Father's Journey

Early 1900 to mid 1990s, Estonia

I had heard the stories about my parents' experiences in the first half of the 1900s my whole life. At one point, my father wrote some of them down. Our family story is tragically like countless other innocent peoples' stories caught between two horrific powers during World War II. Sadly, our story is not unique. Others were worse. This is our story.

So cast your mind back to 1918 to hear some stories from my father.

Story from my father, Oja Ilmar

On Christmas Eve 1918, in Ambla, Estonia, instead of celebrating, my family and I crouched below the windows inside the thick walls of our barn. The black-and-white cows startled, jumped, and bellowed as the bombs blasted and the machine guns rattled. My mother whispered to me that baby Jesus had been born in a manger—a barn—and that we might also be protected by our faith and our hope. I was three and a half years old.

Late that night, the battle finally ended, allowing us to go carefully back into the house. At last, we could sit down to our traditional Christmas meal of oven-roasted potatoes, sauerkraut, blood sausage, and my mother's freshly baked bread.

Suddenly, Russian troops banged at the door. My father got up and let them in. I heard harsh, loud language from the kitchen. My father and my older brother Arnold spoke to them in Russian. I sensed my mother's and my older sister's fear.

The shouting continued. Four Russians followed Arnold across the kitchen. They passed me as I sat in the doorway that led to my father's cobbler shoemaking workshop. I sat on a *taburet*, which is a three-legged stool. Arnold showed them his blunderbuss—an old, half-rusted, muzzle-loaded hunting rifle. The Russian officer looked at it and shouted something at Arnold. He then turned abruptly to walk away. His heavy, unbuttoned military coat, his *sinel*, swung open and struck me in the face. Its buckles stung as the coattail swept across my cheek.

The Russians asked again if we had any "real" rifles and whether my father and Arnold were members of the Estonian National Guard—the Kaitseliit. My father answered "НЕТ" ("no") to both questions. But, he and Arnold were indeed members of the Kaitseliit (National Guard). They both had military rifles hidden away.

After the soldiers left, my father quickly went to the *rehetuba*, the large threshing room next to the living area of our house. He found his army rifle, which was hidden under the floor planks. From the loft, Father got a big bag of straw, which we used to make mattresses, and stuffed the rifle into the bag. He then carried the bag across our yard to the cow barn, where he hid the gun, still securely inside the big bag of straw.

During this house-to-house search, twelve men from our town admitted to being members of the Kaitseliit and having forbidden arms. They were all arrested and taken to Rakvere, a nearby city. Their bodies were later found in a mass grave. All of them had been tortured, their hands tied behind their backs with barbed wire, shot, and tossed into a long trench.

That same Christmas night, long after dinner, suddenly our front door flew open. We froze, fearing the Russians had returned. But instead, in the doorway stood my uncle Ruudi, my mother's brother. He had been in the middle of Ambla village when a gun battle broke out.

Ruudi had tied the reins of his horse to the rain gutter downspout at the firehouse and hid in the stone firehall building. When the shooting stopped, Ruudi used the lull to make his break. Pulling his horse behind him, he ran along the road and made it to the stone bridge at the Ambla River. As he crossed, gunshots rang out again from both sides—Ruudi was stuck in the crossfire. Several bullets hit his newly purchased young horse, dropping it to the ground. Ruudi jumped over the far edge of the bridge and slid down the muddy, steep river bank. There he lay motionlessly as the battle raged, bullets whizzing just above his head. When the fighting finally ended, he scrambled from the riverbank and sprinted to our house.

Ruudi had been born with one leg shorter than the other, which was made worse by an unsuccessful surgery. This caused him to wobble wildly from side to side as he walked. I now watched as he staggered back and forth across the room, telling us what he had just lived through at the Ambla Bridge.

Uncle Ruudi was a great storyteller. In later years, he would regale people with his story of being caught in the middle of the Ambla battle in 1918. Ruudi told how, while lying on his stomach on that river bank, his greatest concern was that if he were shot to death, he would never know who had won—the Russians or the Estonian freedom fighters.

Ruudi sold the hide of his dead horse to a tannery, hoping to recoup some of the money he had just spent buying it. He could only sell the portion that had not been riddled with bullet holes. The horse's tail Ruudi kept for himself. He made a broom out of it by attaching a long handle. For years afterward, Ruudi joked that he could smell the strong scent of money filling his space whenever he swept his room with his horsetail broom.

But as Ruudi told his story that night, the battle erupted again. Bombs boomed. Guns rattled. My father ordered us all to hide behind the large stove in the *rehetuba*, the threshing room, shouting to us, "*Laske kõhuli! Laske kõhuli!*" ("Lay down on your stomachs!")

I do not remember my mother clearly. I remember her funeral, during the winter of 1921. I was only four and half years old at the time. She had become ill and was taken to a large hospital in the capital city of Tallinn. She had some cancer and had undergone surgery but died shortly after that.

My eldest brother Arnold and my uncle Ruudi went to Tallinn with two horses and our sleigh to pick up her body. It was March. The weather was changeable. Cold and snowy days were followed by warmer ones, causing the narrow roads to become rutted and muddy, with dry patches that the horses struggled to drag the sled over. During this trip, though, the weather was freezing.

On their way back, Arnold and Ruudi went into a coffee shop for some hot tea to warm themselves. But Ruudi had failed to tie the horses securely to the post in front of the shop. When they came back outside, the horses and the sled with my mother's coffin were gone.

Perhaps the horses in that freezing weather wanted to return home to their warm stable and fresh hay. Ruudi and Arnold ran, walked, and ran again for quite a long distance before they finally found the horses with the sled stuck in the ditch. A dry patch of ruts in the road may have caused the sleigh to slide into the ditch. The two men pushed as hard as they could, struggling to finally get the sled back onto the dirt road.

The road was narrow, and when other horse-drawn sleighs happened to meet, the drivers would have to gingerly move over to the side, allowing the sleighs to pass each other slowly. One can only imagine what others thought upon seeing a team of horses pulling an empty sleigh containing only a wooden coffin, moving along the muddy, snow-covered road.

My grandmother's funeral (March 1921). #1 Arnold; #2 Alviine; #3 Kustav; #4 my father, Ilmar; #5 Ottomar; #6 my great uncle Ruudi

I cannot clearly remember what my mother looked like or her face. But I still recall the night when the Russian soldier's heavy military metal coat buckles slapped across my face on that Christmas Eve in 1918.

In 1934, as a nineteen-year-old, I moved from Ambla in the center of Estonia, where I had been born, to Linnamäe on the West Coast. Our uncle (my mother's brother) Aleksander Silm drove us to the place I had just purchased with my brothers Arnold and Ottomar. It was a bankrupt mill with a vast manor house and outbuildings surrounded by about seventy acres of land.

After we arrived, I was forced to make a life-altering decision. Uncle Aleks, who was visiting Estonia after having lived in the States for a while, asked me if I wanted to stay in Estonia or go back to America with him and Liisette, who had never had children of their own. When I was six, Aleks and Liisette had wanted to adopt me and take me to America after my mother died. My older sister Alviine resisted this idea at that time. Following my mother's death, Alviine, who was thirteen years older than me, stepped into my mother's role. She was totally against my going to America, so she refused to let me go. However, my older brother Ottomar did go with them to America with them. Now, as a young man just starting a new life in western Estonia, I had to make this huge fateful decision for myself. I decided to stay in Estonia.

At first, living in the new place on the coast worried me. I didn't know whether I'd feel welcomed and comfortable. I worked long hours in our mill, which consumed most of my days and nights. As a young man, I wanted to get out and about to meet young people like me.

In this effort, I became involved with the Linnamäe local community. I joined the local Estonian National Guard unit, the volunteer fire department, and the learned society. These groups organized big parties and social events to cover their operating costs through ticket sales to such events. This circumstance led to a lot of good times and some drinking and carousing.

One effort to become a member of my new community was volunteering to be Santa Claus at the local school. One by one, the students approached me, sat on my knees, and told me what they wanted for Christmas. Even the upper-class students took part in this ritual. One older teenage girl stood out. She wore a yellow dress and had soft green eyes and linen-locked, golden blond hair. She sat on my knee and whispered her wishes to me.

Later, I also joined the Linnamäe theater group, which presented several plays each season. This thespian group consumed most of my free time. I sometimes found myself memorizing three scripts at once for our performances.

Members of the theater group included the brothers Alfred and August Schönberg, who were themselves athletes and organized sporting events in the area. But among the other members was that green-eyed, golden-haired girl, Miralda Laanepere, who had sat on my knee. She had graduated from the local school and was furthering her education nearby Haapsalu.

We grew friendly. I rode my bicycle as often as possible to Miralda's home, Aru Talu (Aru farm), in nearby Vedra Küla. At first, her family was not keen on me coming over so much and being interested in her. Miralda's mother asked her, "Why are you spending time with that Rakfeldt boy from the Räägu flour mill? He isn't all that tall. He has brown eyes and dark hair. Why not get to know the Schönberg brothers better? They are bigger, taller, and more athletic. They also have blond hair and blue eyes." Despite this, I persisted and somehow prevailed.

But the times were coming to a crisis. Twenty-one years after that fateful Christmas in 1918, in 1939, the Nazi–Soviet Pact allowed the Soviets to occupy Estonia once more. I was completing my two-year mandatory service in the Estonian army, which was based in Narva on the Russian border.

By 1940, thousands of Russian troops were already on bases in Estonia. We lived in constant fear, insecurity, and uncertainty.

Miralda and I decided to at least find some stability by getting married. On June 7, 1940, in a civil service performed by the Oru town secretary, Eduard Jõe, we were officially registered as a married couple in the town hall.

Immediately after the official event, along with others who happened to be in the building, we raised our glasses to toast ourselves formally as newlyweds.

Miralda's parents wanted us to also have a religious wedding. On August 31, 1940, we had a small religious ceremony in Kaarli Kirik (St. Charles Church), one of the biggest and most beautiful churches in Tallinn, the capital city. When Miralda's older brother Volli and his live-in girlfriend Linda learned of our plans, they joined us for a double wedding ceremony. It was beautiful, with a few friends and family present.

On the way home in a streetcar that we rode to the train station, my father Kustav Rakfeldt managed to get everyone on board laughing at his funny jokes and stories. Sitting in that tramcar holding hands with my bride that night, I laughed at my father's stories.

I felt satisfied, fulfilled, and deeply loved by my green-eyed, golden-locked girl.

My father doing his compulsory service in the Estonian army (1937–1939).

Russian troops entering Estonia based on the Nazi–Soviet Pact.

Volli and Linda got married too as a double wedding.

Ilmar and Miralda's wedding day (August 31, 1940).

Chapter 8

Hope for Seeing Homeland

August 1973

The sun shone brightly in mid August 1973 in the Muskoka Lakes region of Ontario, Canada. I was again at MÜ, having lunch with my friends, when Henno Sillaste, one of the organizers, announced that the MÜ was scheduled to be held in Finland the following year, 1974. He added that they hoped to secure visas for those interested to take a ten-day trip to Estonia following the MÜ conference. A travel agency in Toronto with good ties to the Soviet authorities would organize the submission of documents.

I couldn't believe what I was hearing. After spending time in Finland, I could safely travel to Estonia with a group. Surely, my parents wouldn't object to that! Henno's announcement sent a buzz through the entire group. I eagerly discussed the trip with my friends Jaan Pill and Tõnu Onu. But still, my parents' concerns and warnings loomed in my mind.

For the rest of the week-long seminar, we were all consumed by the prospect of going to Finland and Estonia the following summer. During dinner and later around the bonfire, we discussed who might attend MÜ in Finland.

I returned to my seven-by-seven tent late that night and crawled into my sleeping bag. I had a hard time falling asleep. My mind was filled with images of going to Finland, Sweden, and Estonia. It felt like when I was a kid and I would lie awake on the night before the annual Harrison radiator company picnic.

Herbert Harrison invented the modern automotive radiator and founded the Harrison Radiator Company in 1910 near us in Lockport, New York. My parents worked at Harrison's, a General Motors factory that made GM cars' radiators and air-conditioning units. The annual picnic was held at Krull Park in Olcott, New York, overlooking Lake Ontario. The amusement park rides and a barbecue lunch with ice cream and goodies for the kids were fantastic. We wore Harrison's tags, which allowed us to ride as often as we wanted for free.

Alone in my tiny tent, I was an excited, giddy kid thinking about going to Finland, Sweden, and Estonia. But my parents' possible negative reaction distressed me.

On my way home from Canada, I stopped at my parents' just across the U.S. border and told them about possibly going with MÜ to Finland and Estonia. Once again, their concerns were raised. But this time, it would be different, as I explained, "*Ma ei lähe üksi, vaid olen osa suurest seltskonnast.*" ("I'm not going alone but as part of a big group.") The trip would be organized by an international travel agency in Toronto that was directly affiliated with the Soviet Intourist officials. I wouldn't have to do all the paperwork myself. I would blend in with this group of others from North

America and be less noticed. Henno had also stressed that the group needed permission and visas, which meant nothing was certain.

Because I taught at a college, my summers were free. I explained to my parents that I could spend time in Finland and Sweden before MÜ, where I could visit my parents' friends from when we lived in those countries.

My parents grudgingly agreed to this plan if we got permission to visit Estonia. At that point, it was unclear whether the Estonian leg would even happen, which took the heat off the need to decide anything immediately.

I headed back to central New York along the New York Thruway with the top down in my Karmann Gia. All the while, my mind was flooded with the idea of spending the following summer in Northern Europe, with a visit to Estonia to cap it off. Visions of Estonia flashed through my head as a fairy-tale place with ancient fortresses, tall turreted towers, narrow cobblestone streets, lakes, and bogs along the Baltic coast dotted by hundreds of islands. The five-hour drive home flew by with me hardly noticing. The soft August breeze blew through my hair. The sun warmed my face and head. I was that giddy kid on the night before Harrison's picnic again.

Chapter 9

From Soviet to Nazi to the Second Soviet Occupation

Summer 1941, Estonia

But my parents had more to tell me about what things were like there. They reminded me of when the Germans betrayed their allegiance to Stalin by attacking the Soviet Union during the summer of 1941.

Many Estonians initially felt relieved by the German betrayal of the Soviets. During the Russian occupation, countless Estonians were murdered and raped, tens of thousands of innocent families were deported to remote labor camps, and thousands of Estonian men were conscripted into the Red Army. Now, the German army was driving the brutal Russian occupiers out of the country. After such horror, anything seemed preferable. There was hope that a free and independent republic could be reestablished.

These hopes, however, were soon dashed. Hitler had his own brutal vision for the Baltic region. He planned to deport the native Estonian population into Russia and replace it with ethnic Germans. Hitler's goal was to make the Baltic Sea into a Germanic

Lake. Germans would be living along the east coast and Germanic language speakers such as the Danes and Swedes along the west coast. This vision was part of Hitler's fundamental ideology to expand Aryan Germans throughout this region and to form a more extensive, larger German *Lebensraum* ("living space").

My father had been a member of the Estonian army, completing his compulsory military service at the onset of the first Soviet occupation in 1940. Possibly because of this, along with the fact that they lived in a large manor house, my parents were on the list to be arrested, deported, or potentially executed. Rather than wait for their fate, they and other friends and family who were at risk of arrest fled into the vast bogs, wetlands, and forests of Western Estonia. After the Germans drove the Soviets out of Estonia in 1941, my parents returned to their home, Räägu Manor, and tried to resume a somewhat normal life under the new occupation.

Like most manors, Räägu was surrounded by a beautiful park. It also had outbuildings, barns, stables, and a large flour mill. The mill provided most of the income they used to pay their mortgage. Estonia is somewhat smaller than the state of Maine, with about the same population. But unlike Maine, because Estonia is surrounded by so much water, it has a temperate climate.

In Räägu, there were large fields planted with various crops and extensive gardens. During the German occupation, the family sold produce and pork raised on the farm to the new occupiers—for a minimal price. The German eastern war front stretched from the Baltic to the Black Sea, so the Germans badly needed locally produced food for their army. This factor may explain why my father was not drafted into the German army, as were so many other

Estonian men. Later, as the war turned against the Germans, they conscripted much older and younger men, often sent to the front only to become cannon fodder. Two choices are offered when drafted: Go to war or take a bullet to the head. Understandably, given such options, many reluctantly went.

One day during the fall of 1941, my father's sister Alviine, the sister who had primarily raised him after his mother died so young, tearfully contacted him, begging him to come immediately. When Isa arrived at her place, he learned that Nazis had come to their door and had broken it open. They had dragged her husband Rudolf Nugis into a nearby field, where they shot him to death. Alviine was shattered by this, and Isa himself was overcome by the grief of losing his brother-in-law and empathized with Alviine's pain and agony.

Given this terror and the widespread insecurity and fear everyone felt, my parents tried to maintain as low a profile as possible during the German occupation. Whenever they dealt with the Germans, they were polite and deferential. The Germans needed their continuous supply of farm produce, which probably kept my family safe.

By that time, the Jewish population in Estonia only numbered about four thousand. In the Czarist Russian Empire, Estonia fell outside of the pale, which were areas in which Jews were allowed to settle and live. Perhaps because of the tiny Jewish population, antisemitism was not prevalent. Indeed, in 1925, as I described previously, Estonia was the first country to legislate providing state support for Jewish cultural autonomy, which meant financing their religious and cultural organizations, schools, and institutions. This legislation is even more remarkable given how such minorities were often treated in Europe during this time.

Fearing the well-known and increasingly clear Nazi ideology, many Jews fled, along with the retreating Russians, before the arrival of the Germans. Sadly, those who remained probably perished. The Nazis added to their atrocities by bringing Jews from other conquered countries and placing them into camps they established in Estonia.

All this horror added to the fear and trepidation felt by all. This cruel reality of invasion and conquest had been the fate of this tiny nation for seven hundred years. The twentieth century stood out as having been both painful and joyful: joyful in that Estonia enjoyed intervals of freedom and independence, but painful from the horrors of three back-to-back occupations, which led to the loss of twenty-five percent of the population. The percentage of Estonians in the country plummeted from 95 to about 60 percent of the total population under the yoke of the occupations.

Due to all this history, my parents were still afraid of what might happen if I were to go back to the country itself. They hadn't been there in thirty years so had no way of knowing what life was like there or if it was safe. And the media in the West was heavily skewed toward making the Soviets out to be horrifically dangerous and cruel. Movies like *The Manchurian Candidate*, political unrest about the Vietnam War and Cuba, and the new hit TV show *M*A*S*H* painted communists as cruel sadists who let nothing stand in the way of their ideology. To my parents, communists were evil, World War II had never really ended, and their beloved homeland was occupied territory. To send me into what they conceived of as a maelstrom frightened them to no end.

Ema especially had vivid memories of her flight from Estonia with her husband and their two young daughters. On Saturdays, when we were young, my older sisters Helle and Tiia and I took baths in an oval-shaped galvanized steel tub filled with water heated on the cast-iron kerosene kitchen stove. My sisters went first, and I took my turn with lukewarm, used water. Once, Helle splashed water in the tub, creating waves, and talked out loud about being in a Baltic storm. My mother sat down, gazed off momentarily, took a breath, and began her story of their flight from Estonia in September 1944.

Chapter 10

Fight from Home: My Mother's Journey

September 1944, Estonia

Major Kõrgmaa crashes through the door. His face is red. He catches his breath. He shouts, "Get ready! I've got a truck. We're going to Noarootsi. There's a boat waiting for us."

God! What should I do now? I am just twenty-two, a young wife and mother. *I'll leave everything behind, fleeing from home, running for my life!*

I grab what I can and stuff my daughters Tiia and Helle into their clothes. My husband Ilmar pushes photos and important papers into a box.

"I'll bury these outside between the big oaks behind the house," he says. "We'll get them when we come back."

We look at each other for a moment. Our eyes freeze. Ilmar's sad brown eyes stare back at me. *Will we come back at all?* I think. *This is no time to let feelings slow us down.* My mind races. *What to take? What to leave? What will we need? I don't even know where we're going; how can I know what to bring?*

Hilda, Arnold (Ilmar's brother), and their children are already outside. Ilmar comes back and shouts, "Let's go, let's go! There's no time. There's no time."

The girls put on coats, mittens, and hats. It's almost October, and it's cold. We go out into the yard. The open truck is packed with people.

How can I just leave everything like this? I haven't even said goodbye to my mother, to my family, to anyone.

The words of my mother then come back to me. The last time I saw her, she said, "Go! Go! You can't stay. They'll kill Ilmar. They'll send you to a slave labor camp."

She was right. She'll understand that I couldn't say goodbye. She'll understand. Tears stream down my face. I can't let the children see these. I wipe them into my blouse sleeve.

We climb up into the truck. I squeeze into the corner. Two-year-old Tiia sits on my lap. Three-year-old Helle sits next to me, looking up into my face. *I hope she didn't see the tears.*

Ilmar climbs into the box of the truck. He squeezes my shoulder. He wears a dark-blue jacket and a hat. *He never wears hats.* I see a scarf around his neck. *He's ready for a cold trip across the Baltic.* I don't even have time to see what he is doing, I am so busy with the girls and my own packing. He quickly shows me the black revolver in his pocket so the others can't see. "We'll be all right," he assures me.

The truck moves slowly out toward the road. For a moment, I almost look back, but instead, I stare straight down at my feet. *Make yourself numb*, I say over and over again, *numb, numb. Now's not the time to feel anything.*

We drive to Linnamäe and turn left toward Noarootsi Beach. Soon we'll pass my childhood home. I stare at the floor more intensely. I sense the truck slowing. I look up to see my sixteen-year-old younger brother Bernhard standing by the roadside. He's holding a loaf of bread for us. The truck doesn't stop. He runs after us. Someone shouts to the driver to stop. "There's no time," the driver yells back. Bernhard runs faster but falls farther behind. I wave. He waves back. His light blond hair blows in the wind. Despair fills his face as tears well up in his green eyes. I sob. Tears burst through even as I struggle to hold them back.

A red glow fills the horizon to the north as the capital city of Tallinn burns. I hear gunfire from the front, which is perhaps only ten kilometers away. *The driver's right—we don't have time to stop*, I tell myself.

At the beach, dozens of people wait, some sitting on huge chests and suitcases, others with nothing at all in their hands, all wanting to get on the three remaining boats.

I grab Tiia and Helle and lower them to Ilmar, who is standing behind the truck. I jump to the ground, clutching our suitcase. Major Kõrgmaa ushers us toward a boat tied to a small pier. People shout and argue about who gets to go. Clearly, all of us won't fit.

Kõrgmaa says, "Rakfeldt must come. The Russians will kill him. His family needs a spot."

What a relief. But it's also hard to see people fighting, begging, pleading, and doing whatever they can to get onto the boats.

Ilmar pushes me forward. I climb toward the low cabin with the girls. Before I stoop below the cabin roof to find a place, I notice Haapsalu burning across the bay. Soviet planes have swept in and bombed the city with its harbor. *That's why they brought us way out here. Haapsalu Harbor's too dangerous.*

A deep, red-colored clay covers the floor of the boat. Cigarette butts, burnt matches, and wood shavings float in the water. I listen to the men talking as we prepare to leave.

One says, "The *Ahti* [our boat's name] was in Tallinn Harbor and a mortar shell exploded next to her. She took shrapnel through the side and sank. She was at the bottom of the harbor for at least a year before they brought her up and fixed the hole."

This explains the cigarette butts, burnt matches, and wood shavings. The workmen butted their cigarettes in here when they fixed the hole, and nobody bothered, or had time, to clean it up. That's why there's all of this red clay caked to the walls too. *God, we're going across the sea, more than two hundred kilometers, in a boat that somebody just pulled up from the bottom of the harbor.* I shudder.

They crank the motor over and over, but it won't start. In the chaos, someone put diesel fuel into the gasoline tank. Someone shouts, "First, we need gas to start the engine. When it's warm, we switch to diesel."

This all takes time. Tempers flare. Shouts and cursing come from the engine area. I see what's going on from my seat. Tiia sits in my lap. Helle's crunched up against me. People are packed in, pressed against each other. Ilmar is outside helping with the motor.

I hear the men say that we're waiting for a naval lieutenant, who will be our captain and take the wheel. He was here earlier but went back to Haapsalu to get his wife. Some say we can't wait anymore. It's getting dark. Finally, Saldvar, who had once been a sea scout, volunteers to take the wheel. Luckily Saarits, a refugee on the boat, had been a mechanic on a ship and is able to start the motor. The compass, however, is stuck. The glass is so discolored from being underwater that Saldvar couldn't read it even if it worked.

As we wait, my sister-in-law Hilda suddenly gets up and says, "We're not going on this boat. Look at this." She points to the water on the floor. "We'll all drown. We won't make it to Sweden. I had a dream that Arnold was out plowing a field. I was in the house with the children, when all at once, the walls fell on us. Dreams are prophetic. We're not going."

I watch helplessly as she pulls her two daughters and son along with her and they get off the boat. Others who had been standing on the shore happily scramble into their vacant places.

Ilmar joins me with a dark face. We do not know if we will see them again.

Soon we are actually moving. Fear and relief fill me. With Saldvar at the helm, the boat moves out toward the open sea. There is a strong thump as we hit a sandbar. The wooden boards push up and water seeps through them.

My God. Now we're stuck. We haven't even gotten out of the bay and we're in trouble. Men climb overboard to push us free. The water's cold. *I hope Ilmar doesn't go in. He'll freeze on the way to Sweden.*

While we're stuck, it becomes clear that there's not enough room for everyone to sit. The floor sloshes with dirty water, so we get ropes and tie suitcases to the cabin's roof. This gives us more room.

Soon, the men push us free, and we're moving again. The engines of the other two boats on the beach won't start at all, so we decide to tow them behind the *Ahti*. However, the *Ahti*'s structure is weakened from having sunk before, so we tie long ropes around her bow leading back to the other two boats. With two boats in tow, we slowly make our way out from the shelter of the bay, staying close to the islands to avoid being spotted by planes or submarines. Finally, we break into the open sea and head west.

The wind picks up right away, and the waves swell. Without a compass, we point the *Ahti*'s nose right into the wind, which is blowing west-southwest. This should lead toward Sweden. The *Ahti*'s engine labors. At times, waves break over the top of the boat. Luckily, Saarits had the foresight to tie an old tent over the top of the cabin, which helps us stay dry.

The motor keeps stalling. We're so overloaded, pushing the stern so low, that when the motor stops, water splashes up into the exhaust pipe and douses the engine. Each time, Saarits pulls the motor's head off to dry it, while a man leans over the stern and closes off the exhaust pipe with his leather hat. Whenever we lose power, the *Ahti* turns sideways and waves lift us high and then drop us suddenly, sometimes ten meters or more.

In this storm, we clearly can't keep pulling the other boats, so the men drag them close to us and the passengers climb onto the *Ahti*, overloading us even more. We then cut the other boats free.

With more than fifty people now on the *Ahti*, there's no place for many to sit. Some cling to the walls of the cabin. Since most are now sick from the storm, the floor sloshes with filthy water, now filled with vomit and excrement along with the clay, cigarette butts, and burnt matches. People had brought enough water for only one day. We've now been out three days. Packs of food remain untouched.

Although warned not to do so, some drink seawater. One older man from Narva suddenly gets up, pushes aside the tent cover, says, "The general is going for his morning swim," and rolls overboard. He disappears into the waves before anyone can grab him. Later, a woman yells, "Stop the bus! Stop the bus! I've got to go to the bathroom. Stop the bus! I've got to piss." She tries to climb over the edge too, but others quickly pull her back.

With Tiia on my lap and Helle clutching my arm, I feel endless movement, up-down, up-down, up-down. All at once, I sense that we've stopped, that we're resting on the bottom of the sea. It feels like our ordeal is over. I feel calm. I don't know how long this lasts. I lose all sense of time.

Suddenly, I hear shouting. Aldvaak has grabbed an automatic rifle and is yelling: "Why prolong our agony? We're all going to die anyway! I'm going to shoot holes into the floor. Let's end this now!" Major Kõrgmaa slowly calms Aldvaak, who gives up his gun and sinks into the corner. His face is a greenish-yellow color. His eyes are vacant. This wakes me from my trance.

Again, there's constant movement. Still, the water pours in from above and from between the boards below. Ilmar uses a bucket to bail out the cabin. Others use tin cans, whatever they can find. But the filthy water keeps rising.

Way up in the bow, a woman cries. She'd been trying to breast-feed her baby. Earlier, the baby had cried constantly. Now, there's silence. The others discuss what to do. My heart freezes as I realize the baby hasn't made a sound. The mother weeps, clutching her baby wrapped in a blanket.

Others say, "We can't keep a corpse on board. It's bad luck. We'll all die." This goes on for some time. Finally, a woman recites a prayer, holding her hands on both the mother and the child. The mother then wraps the baby more tightly in its blanket, kisses it, and hands it to the person sitting next to her, who in turn hands it to the next, and so on, until a man sitting next to an opening gently pushes the baby out into the water. We sit silently.

The next morning, our fourth day at sea, I heard the men shouting. They spotted a ship. We don't know who they are—German, Russian, Swedish—but at last, it's a ship. The storm hasn't let up. Still, the sea pushes us up and then drops us down with a crash. Water splashes over us, over and over again. It seems like forever, but finally, I hear shouts: "*Rootsi! Rootsi!*"

Thank God it's a Swedish ship. If it were Russian, we would have endured all of this only to end up in Siberia anyway.

The Swedes slowly and carefully maneuver next to us to protect us from the waves. They drop rope ladders down to us.

"We'll get the women and children out first!" Kõrgmaa shouts.

A few men atop the cabin are lifted off first, though. I look up and see a wall of gray metal that forms the side of the Swedish ship. As the wave sweeps us up to the level of the deck, the gray wall vanishes as Swedish sailors grab people, pulling them on board. They time it perfectly, grabbing people only when the wave lifts us to their height. Suddenly, I notice Mr. Triumph, the head accountant for the Estonian Bank in Haapsalu, hanging on to the edge of the ship as the wave drops us again. He wears two suits and a heavy winter coat, which he hopes to take with him to Sweden. However, with these wet clothes, he's so heavy that the sailors can't pull him on board. He slips and falls into the water, vanishing beneath the waves.

Stunned, I hand Tiia and Helle up to Ilmar. He then passes the girls up to others, who hand them to the Swedes. At that moment, I think, *My God, are the buttons closed tightly on the big coat wrapped around Helle?* An image flashes through my mind of a sailor grabbing the big loose coat as little Helle slips out and falls between the ships.

Ilmar grabs me. I sit stiffly, unable to move. I can't be budged. He shakes me harder. I try standing. My legs won't work. Someone then pushes me from behind as others pull me forward. I'm dazed. Next, I feel the steel deck under me. Ilmar grabs my arm and pulls me into the cabin; Tiia's lying in a basket. Helle stands next to her, looking up at me.

She says, smiling, "They've got hot chocolate! They've got hot chocolate!"

This is an excerpt from the official naval log of the *Gävle*.

> At 0900, about 3° WSW on Bogskären, just over five kilometers southwest of the southernmost islands of the Åland archipelago, we encountered a ten- to twelve-meter motorboat without a propeller that was drifting uncontrollably. The boat was filled to capacity with people lying or sitting on the deck and below, most of whom appeared to be in a numb, stupor-like state. In the rough seas, the motorboat was at risk of being crushed or overturned. The refugees were gradually pulled and winched one at a time onto the ship by the crew of the *Gävle*, who risked their lives due to the sudden movements of the boat and the naval destroyer. During the rescue, two refugees fell into the water.
>
> (Komandörkapten Bror Fredrik Thermaenius' *Gävle* naval log)

(Göran. A.C. (2004). Sweden and the Great Flight from Estonia 1943–1944. Uppsala.)

(Translated from Swedish by Jaan Seim)

Mother had told me these stories many times. I empathized with their anguish and admired their heroism.

But I had learned so much from MÜ in 1972 and again in 1973 when I returned about Estonia's fervent and undying spirit, which I was sure could not have been completely quelled in the homeland. I needed to experience it for myself. Despite my parents' fears, I decided that 1974 was the year. I decided to go.

My sister Tiia is in the basket at the bottom right. Photo of the *Gävle's* captain above Tiia's photo.

The *Ahti*, with the two smaller boats in tow, leaving for Sweden. During the storm, people from the small boats climbed aboard, overloading the *Ahti* more.

This photo shows their escape. My father is marked.

Nii see algas: Väljasõit Voosi kurgust
Rootsi suunas 24. septembril 1944

On see hr. Ilmar Rakfeldt ?

Arvatavasti viimane foto minu isast

Foto: August Kiidla

This is what the Estonian capital city, Tallinn, looked like during the 1944 Russian onslaught.

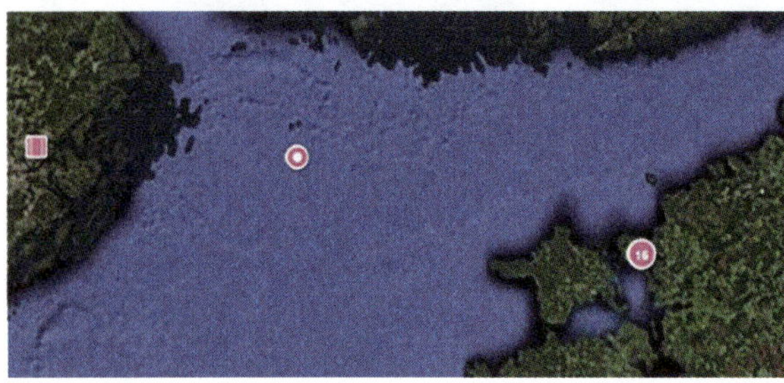

This photo shows where they left Estonia (#16) and where they were rescued four days later in Finnish waters (red dot).

This photo is of the actual rescue.

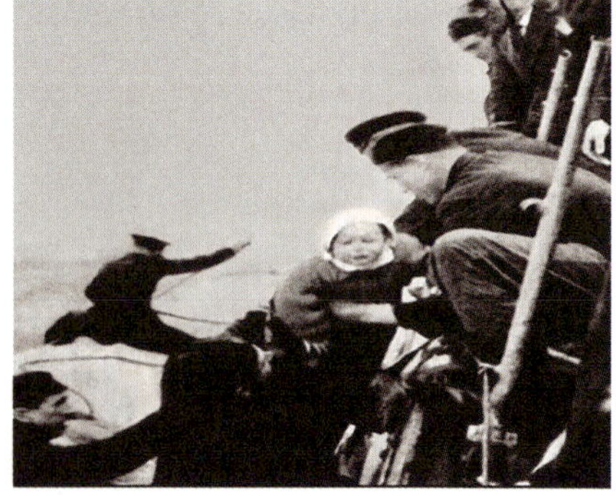

Photo of HMS *Gävle*, the Swedish naval ship that rescued them while the *Ahti* had no power and was sinking.

Chapter 11

My Journey Continues: A New Chapter Unfolds

Summer 1974

I pulled slowly out of the driveway. Isa sat beside me in the front, and Ema sat in the rear seat beside my backpack. She said she couldn't imagine me being in Europe for several weeks with merely a backpack and my camera case, but I said I liked to travel light. I'd taken trips like this before and could certainly do it again.

It's about one hundred miles from Newfane to Toronto International Airport. The trip could take as little as two hours with light traffic, but Toronto traffic is often brutally congested and slow. This time, we left early with plenty of time to arrive, and the trip went well. It was smooth going through customs, and this was when the family could still accompany you to the departure gate. We talked until it was time for me to board.

I was excited and looking forward to my adventure. We discussed what I would be doing and who I would see in Sweden. Isa said that he had contacted friends there, telling them that I would be coming for a visit. We checked to ensure that I had the addresses and contact information for everybody I needed. The prospect of my visiting people who knew us in Stockholm had softened my parents' opposition to my trip. I looked forward to spending time in Finland and attending the MÜ seminar. But it was the idea of going to Estonia for the first time in my life that made my heart leap.

Still, looking severe, Isa adamantly cautioned me that while in Estonia, I was not to contact relatives. I assured him I would stay with the tourist group and avoid creating any problems.

Ema warned me to be careful around Finnish women, saying, "*Soome naised võivad olla võrgutavad ja üritavad sind libedale teele meelitada.*" ("Finnish women may be seductive and try to lure you onto a slippery slope.")

"*Ainult unenägudes,*" ("Only in my dreams") I said, laughing, thinking surely she was joking. But she repeated it more sternly. I shrugged it off, thinking there was no way this would ever happen. I assured her that I'd be careful, as I had been during previous solo trips to England, the Netherlands, Belgium, Germany, and Sweden.

I gave Isa the American Express office address in Helsinki, where I could pick up mail if they needed to contact me. When the call came for me to board my plane, we hugged and said goodbye. Ema kept urging me to be careful, and Isa told me to be upstanding and carry myself in a way I could be proud of myself.

I was happy to have a window seat to see as much as possible. I had been studying the Berlitz Finnish phrase book and dictionary and had learned some essential words and phrases. This was not so hard because Finnish and Estonian are closely related. Because of our square faces, high cheekbones, blond hair, and light-colored eyes, Estonians and Finns look alike.

When the flight attendants spoke to me in Finnish, I proudly responded with my words and phrases such as hello (*hei*), good day (*hyvää päivä*), I will order a beer (*tilaan olu*), a salmon (*tilaan lohta*), and where is the toilet? (*missan on WC?*) and thank you (*kiitos*). The problem was that they would respond by rapidly firing off lengthy phrases, leaving me completely lost. Sheepishly, crest-fallen, I switched to English. But they liked that I tried speaking to them in Finnish, and they were very friendly.

After a few days in Finland, I took the overnight ship from Helsinki to Stockholm. I left around seven at night and arrived in Stockholm early in the morning, passing through an archipelago of small islands, many with cozy cottages.

In the ship's bow was a ballroom with a live band and a wonderful smorgasbord spread with great food. People ate, drank, and danced into the wee hours of the morning. The sea was choppy, and the ship's dance floor rose and fell with the waves, sending dancers colliding against one another, but nobody seemed to mind.

I didn't want to look like a wallflower sitting by myself. Finally, I summoned the courage to ask a young, attractive Swedish lady to dance to slower music. Surprisingly, she pulled herself tightly against me, a total stranger. As we swayed, the ship's rolling pushed us together. That was nice. I escorted her back to her seat in a gentlemanly way and returned to mine. It was fun.

Soon, a tipsy Finnish woman approached me, asking me to dance. Thinking of my mother's warning and seeing the woman's inebriation, I responded, "*Mina en tanssi.*" ("I don't dance.") She kept pulling my hand, insisting. I responded with a warm, friendly smile, slowly shaking my head. "No." Her response was "*Valehtelet minulle*" ("You are lying to me") as she abruptly turned and left.

As things grew more raucous, I went to my cabin below. Walking along the deck, I saw people sleeping on lounge chairs, saving the cost of a cabin. I found my tiny cabin and crawled into bed, feeling good about how things were going. I looked forward to meeting friends in Sweden and seeing Stockholm. Drifting off to sleep, I recalled my airport goodbyes with my parents and smiled, remembering again Ema's warning about assertive Finnish ladies. Perhaps there was something to her concern.

Traveling with a backpack and staying in youth hostels, I spent several weeks in Finland and Sweden before the seminar began. I journeyed to Lapland in the far north, several hundred kilometers north of the Arctic Circle. Upon arrival, after the long train ride from Helsinki, I learned that the only youth hostel was full, so I merely threw my sleeping bag onto the soft, lush vegetation that was there due to the long Arctic summer days and slept under the midnight sun.

A boat took me to the island of Ukonsaari in Lake Inari, which the Sami believe to be a holy place. I saw ancient religious sites as well as a sacrificial cave. The Inari Sami people have lived near this lake for over two thousand years.

I had several encounters with Sami during my trip. Americans tend to know Sami as Laplanders, the nomadic reindeer herders of the North. Their language is like Estonian. Both belong to the Finno-Ugric language family. The winter war, which had begun when the Soviet Union invaded Finland on November 30, 1939, ended on March 13, 1940 with the signing of the Moscow Peace Treaty. The fighting had been fierce in this region, resulting in Karelia, a large area of Finland, being seized and annexed by Russia.

On the train ride to Lapland, a couple of Finns and a Sami man sat in the rear of my train car, passing around a bottle of vodka. As they drank, their speech grew louder and more boisterous. Surprisingly they invited me to join them, which I did. The Sami guy kept loudly shouting, "*Perkele Saksalaiset, Perkele Venäläiset!*" ("To hell with Germans, to hell with Russians!")

Word must have gone ahead of us about what they were doing. At the next train station, uniformed police officers entered our train car and began arresting my companions. A Finn, sitting in front of me, whispered in English. "Don't move. Don't say anything." I sat frozen in my seat, staring forward as the police led my compadres away. I could easily have spent the night in jail in the Finnish city of Oulu near the Arctic Circle on the shore of the Gulf of Bothnia.

On the train back toward Helsinki, I met a Finnish couple, Harri and Gun-Brit, and had meaningful conversations during the long ride. They generously invited me to stay with them for several days in their beautiful home overlooking the Gulf of Finland, with a sauna and an indoor swimming pool. I'm still amazed that they took me into their home and were so kind and generous toward me, a long-haired, bearded, backpacking stranger from America.

During my trip, I listened to my tiny transistor radio, where I learned from Estonian national radio Vikerraadio that U.S. President Nixon had resigned. While in Sweden, I visited people who had known my family from our time there. I even spoke with people who had been on the boat with my parents when they escaped Estonia.

When the MÜ seminar people arrived, I met them at the airport. We boarded a charter bus for the five-hour trip to Kuopio, a beautiful city nestled in the woods of Finland surrounded by several lakes.

I spent a week with the literati of the Estonian exile community from Europe and North America. There were wonderful lectures, discussion groups, singing and dancing opportunities, swimming, bonfires, and a sauna. Each afternoon, a small group gathered at the end of a long pier that jutted out into a clear blue lake surrounded by pristine forest to sing *regilaule*, which are traditional chanting songs, oral poetry sung in a call-and-response style in the same rhythmic meter as the national epics of both Finns and Estonians. These have been sung for centuries. Rein Taagepera, a UC Irvine professor and later an Estonian presidential candidate, led our group.

While there, I also became acquainted with a young woman from Estonia named Silja. While working for Estonian radio, she met, married, and divorced a Finnish basketball player, leaving her in Finland. She told me she planned to visit her grandmother in Estonia while I would be there with my MÜ group.

After the seminar ended, we boarded the ship to Estonia in the Helsinki Harbor. As the ship pulled away from the dock, we waved to those who had been denied visas to enter Estonia by the Soviets. They were *persona non grata*, including Professor Taagepera and Vello Salo, a Catholic priest who was the Estonian language broadcaster on Vatican Radio.

I thought about the last time anyone in my family had been here, on a boat going in the other direction, fleeing Estonia for Sweden. The memories from my parents' stories flooded back to me.

Läänemere lained	Baltic Sea Waves
Seal, kus Läänemere lained laksuvad, seal, kus tuuled, tormid aina mühavad, seal on valge majak, valge nagu luik, seal on minu kodu, seal mu sünnipaik.	There where Baltic Sea waves lap the shore, There where winds and storms oft-times roar, Stands a snug house, white like a swan. This is my birthplace, my life's dawn.

Chapter 12

Starting Over: Refugee Life in Sweden

September 1944

While fleeing Soviet terror in 1944, Estonians were ready to put their lives and their families at great peril. It was an existential dilemma captured in the phrase "*Minna ei taha, kuid jääda ei saa.*" ("We do not want to go but cannot stay.")

Most boats, like the ones my family boarded, were dangerously overloaded. Often, the engines stopped running. Stormy winds smashed the helpless boats up against rocks. No one knows how many ships were lost. Two bigger ships sunk by the Russians alone accounted for about one half of the Estonian casualties.

One was a hospital ship, the *Moero*, marked as such by a big red cross on the roof, which left Tallinn, Estonia on September 21, 1944. Soviet aircraft sank the *Moero*, leading to more than three thousand deaths, primarily women and children.

The second was the *Nordstern*, which left Saaremaa Island on October 3, 1944, with a passenger manifest that was three-quarters women and children. My uncle Arnold was on that boat with his wife Hilda and my three cousins, Milvi, Leili, and Toivo.

As Ema told me, "Once they left our boat, the *Ahti*, they were able to get onto the *Nordstern*, a bigger and sturdier ship. But the Russians torpedoed it, and as Hilda's dream had predicted, only Arnold survived."

Hilda and the children drowned after a Russian torpedo cut the ship in half, causing it to sink in less than two minutes. My uncle Arnold was among the few who survived.

When my parents were rescued by the Swedes, Ilmar's first night in Nynäshamm, a harbor city on the Swedish coast, was spent in a cavernous room in the city's Community Center hall with all the men. Miralda and their daughters were in a nearby church basement with all the other women and children.

These men were the last ones, the final wave of Estonian refugees, to escape before the Soviets cut off the seacoast. Later, a few more people straggled in from the Estonian islands. Because everyone on the boat had been completely soaked with salt water and diesel fuel, all their clothes had to be burned. The Red Cross gave out donated clothing that didn't fit anyone very well, but at least this raiment covered their naked bodies. After feeding and clothing the rescuees, the Swedes gave them sleeping bags made of paper, as well as blankets and pillows.

Sweden was governed by a leftist party and had strong leftist labor unions then. These unions regularly used Nynäshamm Community Center's huge hall for union meetings. On the walls hung posters of Marx, Engels, Lenin, and Stalin, under whose gaze the unions conducted their business. This created the most bitter of ironies. After all, it was Stalin's troops and death squads that had swept across Estonia and from whom these men had just barely managed to escape with their lives.

Ilmar was exhausted, not having slept for more than sixty hours. But despite his fatigue, he couldn't sleep. Bodies in those paper sleeping bags filled the whole floor of the enormous room. During the night, even the slightest movement would make the paper bags crackle loudly.

Lying on the hardwood floor, Ilmar's body twitched, trembled, and cramped inside the crackling bag. He was sad. The years of trying to stay alive had taken their toll. Ever since he had fled into the forest during the summer of 1941, he had felt like a condemned man waiting for execution. It was now September 1944; the horror, the terror, the agony of running and hiding from the death squads and, finally, the ever-approaching battlefront had left deep emotional wounds. He also felt guilty for having fled and abandoned the men who had been with him in the forest.

This was the past, and that was troubling enough. But the future didn't look much brighter. Ilmar now faced the vast unknown of what was to come. He and his young family were now in a strange land, unable to speak a word of the language, with no money and no marketable skills.

Ilmar had been a miller in Estonia, but would these skills do him any good in Sweden? Most recently, he had led the local self-defense unit. As these thoughts passed through his mind, he realized that at least he had not been forced to wear the uniform of any foreign army, as had so many other Estonian men who had been drafted.

Finally, Ilmar lost consciousness and fell into a deep slumber. When he awoke the next day, he noticed that all the posters had been turned inward toward the wall. Someone had silently reversed them. Whoever had done this wanted these refugees to feel safer, sleep, and finally find some peace.

My family was eventually assigned an apartment on Borensvägen Street in the Årsta-Johannesev district, a nice new neighborhood not far from the center of Stockholm. I was born about two years after their arrival, in 1946, on Sunday, August 25, 1946.

That morning was beautiful, around seventy degrees, with natural light flooding our apartment through the large windows facing south. Shortly after breakfast, Ema began feeling discomfort and contractions that grew more frequent and intense. She called her doctor and was told to go to the hospital. Isa ordered a taxi, which arrived shortly. Fortunately, we lived on the first floor, and it was a short stairway to the front door. It wasn't hard for Ema to leave with Isa's help and get into the cab. Helle and Tiia were excited but worried after seeing Ema in such distress.

The Southern Stockholm Hospital (Södersjukhuset) was less than three miles away or about a ten-minute drive on the shore of Årsta Bay (Årstavike). As they drove, the bright sun filtered through the trees, casting beams of light onto the street while church bells chimed on this beautiful Sunday morning, adding a spiritual and supernatural tone.

Suddenly, there was a pop, and the taxi shook, bumped, and rolled to a stop on the side of the road with a flat tire. Isa urged the driver to get closer to the hospital, but he refused.

My parents were forced to get out, and Isa supported Ema while carrying her small suitcase as they slowly made their way forward. The hospital was less than a third of a mile away, but it seemed like miles. Finally, they reached the emergency room entrance. Ema was immediately rushed into a room. Perhaps the walking hastened her labor. I was born immediately and easily.

After Ema brought me home, Tiia and Helle were fascinated by my tiny fingers and toes. Soon, I became like a sideshow attraction, with Tiia and Helle bringing their friends through our apartment to marvel at my little digits.

Ema worked at the textile factory that owned our apartment building and hired many Estonian refugees living there. She began taking in children as daycare during her maternity leave to earn extra money.

At that time, Sweden rationed many consumer items and goods. Even though the war had just ended, beer was still rationed. But beer was believed to provide necessary nutrients for nursing mothers, so vouchers allowed them to purchase more than would normally have been allowed. After a while Ema no longer wanted the beer, so she sold her vouchers to others to earn extra money. I used to joke to my friends that I started drinking beer as an infant through my mother's milk.

My years in Sweden were happy and filled with love and security from my parents, sisters, and the kids in our building. Sweden was a time of joy for me as I basked in the love of my family and friends. I always had kids to play with.

One time, my sisters Helle and Tiia were getting ready to go to the park near our apartment building, where we lived along with many other Estonian refugees, Borensvägen 56. I said I wanted to go along with them, but they said no because there would only be bigger kids at the playground that day. They walked out of the door, down the short flight of stairs to the first-floor entranceway, and out through the main entrance of our apartment building. I ran out onto the balcony, stood on my tiptoes, and watched as they crossed the street and headed toward the nearby park with its fun-looking swings, slides, and jungle gym.

I was so sad about being left home alone that I decided that I would go to the park as well. I put on my shoes and left the apartment, running down the stairs to the front door. Once outside, I started to walk in the direction that I had seen Helle and Tiia go until I came to a wide street.

I remembered the park with its playground because it was one of our favorite places to go, and when I left our home, I was confident I could find it. But where I stood didn't look familiar. I looked for oncoming cars in both directions and dashed across a wide street. I kept walking in what I thought was the direction of the park. Soon, I came upon a big intersection. Once again, I looked around to see what the traffic was doing. When the cars stopped, I ran to the other side of the intersection as fast as possible. Still, nothing looked familiar to me.

I was exhausted from walking, and the hot sun beating down made me even wearier. I didn't know how long I had been on the street or how far I had gone. I decided to give up on the park and try to return to the apartment. Once again, I had to cross the same streets.

As I walked, everything began looking less and less familiar to me. I didn't even remember where I had come from. The sun was hot. I was thirsty. I was exhausted. I began to panic. I couldn't find my way back home.

Suddenly, a tall stranger towered over me. I got scared. He bent down, looked at me, and said something in Swedish. I didn't understand him. I spoke only Estonian.

I tried telling him I got lost while looking for my sisters Helle and Tiia at the park. He just stared at me, and he didn't understand a word of what I said.

All at once, he lifted me off the ground and placed me in his bicycle's front basket. He then jumped onto the bike himself and began riding along the street.

What he didn't know, of course, is that once I had gotten my feet caught in the spokes of my father's bike. I was afraid of bicycles. So now I started to yell, scream, and cry.

The stranger didn't know what to do with me. He kept talking to me, but I didn't understand him. He pulled me out of the basket, then walked along beside me while rolling his bicycle along the sidewalk. I didn't know who this man was or where he was taking me.

After crossing several streets, I finally recognized the market and stores at the end of Borensvägen, near home, where my journey had begun. We turned onto our street. Number 56 was the third building on the left-hand side. A big rock was outside in front of our building, next to the street.

I saw our neighbors and my parents out on the street from a distance. They all looked frantic. Because of my constant crying, they heard me coming from a distance.

My parents ran over to us. In Swedish, the tall stranger told my parents he was a neighbor and had recognized me from when he walked past our building and saw me climbing on the rock with other kids. He had found me several blocks away, standing on a street corner.

My parents both thanked him profusely in Swedish. "*Tack så mycket, tack så mycket!*" ("Thank you so very much, thank you so very much!") My mother picked me up and hugged me. Tears swelled in her soft green eyes. She told me, "*Otsisime sind igast kohast. Olime peaaegu politseisse helistamas.*" ("We looked for you all over the place. We were about to call the police.")

"*See Rootslane oli kena mu vastu,*" I said. ("That Swede was nice to me.")

As recounted earlier, after being brought to the refugee camp in Sweden, my parents immediately applied to immigrate to the United States, but the tiny immigration quota in the States prevented us from going. Moreover, the Swedish government was occasionally cooperating with the Soviet government by sending some Baltic refugees back to the occupied countries to face certain execution or slave labor camp incarceration.

Fear and uncertainty were sweeping through the Estonian refugee community. Some Estonians pooled their money and purchased old, broken-down boats that they fixed up and used for the long, treacherous journey across the Atlantic Ocean. Entire families, men, women, and children spent weeks crowded onto these boats sailing to safety in North America.

This uncertainty and fear led to my parents' desperate decision to go to Canada while they still could.

Nynäshamm's Community Center building, where the men slept on the floor.

Church basement where women and children slept.

My father at work at the textile factory.

My mother at work at the textile factory.

This photo is from a Swedish magazine featuring a story about Estonian refugees. Helle and Tiia are the girls sitting on the big rock on the left. Our apartment was the first one on the first floor, to my sisters' right.

Helle, Tiia, and me in Sweden.

My first Christmas in Sweden. Notice the real candles.

Our family together.

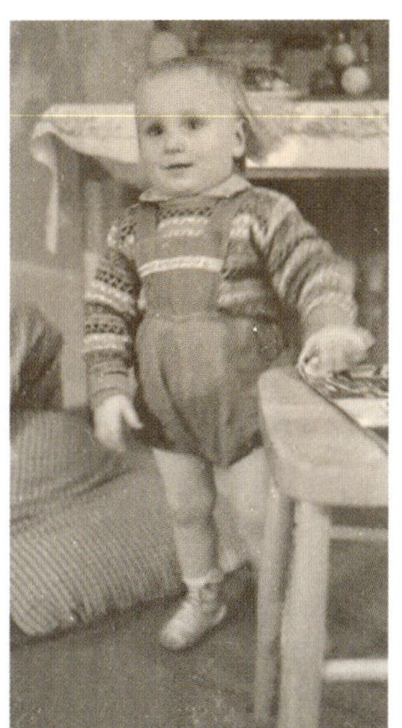

Me in Sweden.

Chapter 13

London

November 1949

Our friends Salum and Rein ran along beside our train. Rein pushed his bike as he ran, waving his free hand goodbye. The train picked up speed, and Rein fell behind. Salum kept pace, waving and shouting, "*Kas peate ikka minema*?" ("Do you have to go?")

It was November 1949. The smoke and steam from the locomotive clouded the train platform in Stockholm. Salum, Rein, and the others who'd come to see us off disappeared into the mist. My parents leaned forward against the windows. My older sisters, Helle and Tiia, stood on the seat, still waving. I sensed something huge happening, though as a little kid, I was too young to understand exactly what. My parents and sisters seemed sad.

We rode for hours to the southern Swedish port of Göteborg, where we boarded a ship for England. I watched as the crate containing our possessions was lifted on board. The winds whipped the North Sea waves. The Swedish ship bounced up and down. Things crashed around me. My world of sunlight and safety in Stockholm was gone. My parents had told my sisters and me that moving to Canada would suit our family, but I wondered: Would it?

Once we arrived, it felt good to be on land again, in England, but my knees wobbled as I tried to keep up with my parents. We boarded a train bound for London. I rubbed my hand along the velvet curtains and seats. The British train was so much nicer than the Swedish ones. We arrived at Victoria Station: huge and ornate, with a high glass ceiling. I'd never seen anything like it.

London was so different from Stockholm. Even the people looked different. Swedes tended to look similar with light complexions, hair, and eyes. The English looked different, with darker hair, while wearing darker clothes. The buildings were dark and soot-covered, black and foreboding. The cars were all black. London didn't even smell like Stockholm. Exhaust spewed from trucks and vehicles, fumes from chimneys. Both filled the dense London air.

My father's brother Arnold met us in front of the station on the street. Arnold was the one who had lost his entire family when the Russians torpedoed their ship. Now he and his new bride Heli hurried toward us, out of breath. They apologized for being late. Heli lifted me from the ground and kissed my face. She had deep-red-colored lips that smudged lipstick onto my cheek. She wore lots of jewelry and smelled strongly of perfume. She was nothing like Swedish women, and nothing like my mother.

So many of the buildings in London were still bombed and burned-out carcasses, massive hulks, from the Blitz in World War II. Intact buildings were blackened by the smoke from years of burning soft coal. London felt foreboding and scary walking along the street, with dark clouds, damp coldness, black and burned-out buildings, and black cars.

In our short time there, my parents took the opportunity to have me christened. St. Peter's Anglican Church, Cranley Gardens, in London, now an Armenian church, was where the London Estonians held their Lutheran services at the time. St. Peter's was dark, chilly, and cavernous. Onu Arnold and his wife Heli became my godparents. Arnold wanted to be my godfather to replace somehow his son Toivo, who was lost when the Russians torpedoed their ship. The Very Reverend Dr. Jaak Taul wore a long black robe with a small white collar. Around his neck, he wore a long chain with a large cross at the end.

My parents, my sisters, and Arnold and Heli stood in the dark, cold, damp church. Reverend Taul spoke to my parents before turning toward me, lifting a bowl of water in his left hand. With his right hand, he made the sign of the cross. I stood directly in front of him, knowing I was about to be baptized. I didn't fully understand what this meant, but I recognized it was exotic, unique, and essential.

I held Ema's hand as he conducted the ceremony. Suddenly, Reverend Taul splashed water on my head—once, twice, three times. While doing this, he recited, "*Isa, poja ja püha vaimu nimel.*" ("In the name of the Father, and of the Son, and of the Holy Spirit.") Drops fell on my nose as he blessed me with water on my forehead. I looked up at Ema and said, "*Üks tilk kukkus nina otsa.*" ("A drop fell on my nose.") Helle and Tiia giggled. My father stood solemnly, while my mother smiled slightly.

After the service, we moved from the altar area to a side room. Reverend Taul opened a big book with heavy dark leather covers to record the christening into the big ledger. He showed me what he wrote. He placed the date in one column, the names of my godparents in another, and in the center, he wrote my name. As he did, he leaned forward and said to me, "*Minu nimi on ka Jaak.*" ("I also have the name Jaak.") I looked at him and said, "*Pane Kaagu ka.*" ("Write Kaagu too.") I also wanted to be remembered by the name the Estonian kids back in Sweden had given me, the name I'd mostly known. Jaak seemed too formal for a three-and-a-half-year-old. (During a trip to London many years later in 1988, I telephoned Dr. Taul, who read to me what he had written. It did not include Kaagu.)

Arnold and Heli hugged me and said they were happy to be my godparents. They looked sincerely pleased. Walked back toward our hotel, we rounded a corner, and I saw a hurdy-gurdy man and his monkey. What joy! The music, the monkey, all out on this street! I ran ahead of the others to get a closer look. The monkey wore a bright red jacket and a small round hat. With a tiny tin cup in its hand, it jumped up onto the hurdy-gurdy box that the man was cranking. It then leaped onto the man's shoulder, and finally, back down onto the street. I wanted to stay there and watch the monkey's antics and listen to the happy hurdy-gurdy music. But my parents pulled me forward, and we continued toward our hotel.

As we walked, I noticed a black car down below the level of the street. It looked like it was in a cellar. I wondered how the car could ever have gotten down there and how they'd ever get it back out. (Maybe it was an underground parking lot.) Across the street was the carcass of a bombed-out building: the façade standing, the inside hollow. Uncle Arnold explained that many such buildings were left in London from the Nazi bombing raids.

At the hotel, we met fellow Estonians Mr. and Mrs. Koidu, who lived in London, and Mr. and Mrs. Nurming, who were on their way to Canada too. My father pulled a bottle of vodka from his suitcase. He explained to the others how Sweden strongly restricted alcohol sales, so there was a thriving black market. Each month we could only buy alcohol by showing government-issued coupons, and we earned extra spending money by selling our coupons to others. He laughed. "I sold a small bottle of vodka in Sweden for twice its price. I bought this big tax-free bottle on the ship from Sweden with the extra kroner." He proudly opened the bottle, raised his glass, and toasted my having been christened. Then, all the adults toasted at the reunion.

My parents and Arnold had not seen each other in five years, not since September 1944 when Arnold's wife made them leave our wooden boat bound for Sweden. Arnold would never recover from their loss, but now, at least, he and my father were together again, and he was starting over with his Heli.

A small party started with talking, laughing, and even singing. Joy filled the hotel room. In Estonia, Heli had been a singer. She had performed and sung professionally. She led the others in song. No one seemed to care that we were in a hotel room in the middle of London. The talking, laughter, and singing lasted until almost dawn. My sisters and I finally fell asleep on the bed.

The next morning, we rode in a black British cab to Paddington Station. It also had a glass ceiling that again amazed me. We took a Great Western Railway train south from London to Southampton. At the harbor pier, we boarded the British ocean liner, the RMS *Aquitania*, for our seven-day trip across the North Atlantic. It was a huge, originally coal-burning converted to oil, four-funneled ship—a member of the Cunard-White Star line. It was one of the great floating palaces built in 1914. As we boarded, though, I still wondered, *Is our going to Canada really a good idea?*

A bombed-out building in London.

St. Peter's Cranley Gardens, London, England. The place of my baptism on November 14, 1949.

Silver cup was given to me by Arnold and Heli on the occasion of my christening, November 14, 1949, in London.

The Very Reverend Dr. Jaak Taul.

Chapter 14

Storms at Sea, Challenges at Landing: Starting Anew in Canada

My memories of crossing the ocean to Canada still crowd my mind. The North Atlantic was stormy and treacherous in late November, but this was when cheap tickets for cramped cabins were available for people like us.

The huge ship tossed up and down constantly—thump, thump, thump, thump, thump, thump, thump. I lay on the top bunk listening to the big cylinders. The smell of the ship filled my nostrils—a sweet antiseptic odor. Below, in the small room, the men played cards and drank. The bottles and glasses clinked and clattered as the big ship rose and fell—thump, thump, that-ta, thump, thump.

The antiseptic smells mixed with the aroma of tomato soup left standing. Someone lurched over to one of the boxes attached to the wall and threw up. The sounds of his dry heaves broke the rhythm of the engines. The storm raged for the whole trip. It was seven days of such smells and sounds, watching men drink, puke, and drink again, and always the huge cylinders chunk-thump, that-ta, thump, thump.

A man sat at the end of the table, drinking evaporated milk from tin cans. He thought it was coconut milk and insisted that others drink it too. He said it would keep one healthy and prevent seasickness. Soon he too lurched toward the box on the wall.

We walked through a large ballroom. My hand limply held on to my mother's. The floor moved under my feet, pushing up under me, and then sharply, suddenly dropping. I saw a crystal ashtray sliding across a table as we passed it. Reaching up, I let go of my mother's hand, grabbed the ashtray, and stood frozen to the table, holding on with all my might, trying to prevent this shiny crystal from falling to the floor. But while I was distracted by this, my family disappeared into the crowd.

I panicked. I felt abandoned and scared, but I didn't want the glass ashtray to fall. I watched as the others walked away from me, leaving me standing with one hand on the table, clutching the ashtray. I wanted to run after them but was afraid to let go—afraid the ashtray would crash to the floor as our dishes had earlier. I stood frozen.

But then I saw Ema break through the crowd with her arms stretched toward me. She saw me wearing my gray hat with flaps covering my ears and a round cloth ball on top, crying and holding the ashtray. She smiled, picked me up, and showed me that the table had small edges to keep things from sliding off. Warm, soothing relief flooded through me while in Ema's arms.

When I reluctantly let go of the ashtray and we hurried to catch up with the others, I looked back to see the ashtray again sliding back and forth across the table but not falling due to the table's edges.

My trying to save this ashtray was utterly absurd when, at the same time, and all the while, the ship's staff and some of the other passengers were destroying everything. They broke off chunks of the ornate, finely handcrafted woodwork. A steward pulled down massive crimson drapes. Like crows on carrion, people cut these curtains into pieces and stuffed them into their pockets and bags. I was dazed by such destruction. People tore off souvenirs from this famous ship because this was the *Aquitania*'s final Atlantic crossing before being scrapped. We didn't get anything, though. Perhaps, because this was its last trip and because the November crossing is so challenging through the stormy North Atlantic, the staff was arrogant and obnoxious. The crew didn't care much about the passengers' comfort and well-being. In particular, the staff mistreated Jews. They showed disdain when dealing with special food requests and complaints about cabin conditions.

Finally, we arrived in Nova Scotia. It was dark as we eased up to Pier 21 in Halifax Harbor. Once more, I marveled at the size of the ship—it was so high, so wide, so full of narrow passages, which then opened onto huge ornate staterooms and ballrooms.

Other passengers scurried off to meet people greeting them onshore, but we weren't allowed to go. Uniformed Canadians looked over our documents. There was a problem. They didn't let us off the ship. My father explained to them, first in Swedish and then in German, that an apartment was already available to us in St. Catharines, Ontario, and that people there would vouch for us. But the officials kept shaking their heads.

Then my father pointed to his passport, showing he was carrying over $3,000 in Canadian money. "Surely, we can get started with this!" he implored. This was a lot of money in 1949. My father carried cash as a courier for others who planned to immigrate later. Sweden restricted the amount of currency persons could take when leaving the country. My father had agreed to deposit this money in a bank; his cut was 10 percent. He hoped this ploy would work. It didn't. The Canadians refused to let us go. Finally, my father tried calling his brother in the States but couldn't get through.

They led us away to a sizeable warehouse-like building right on the harbor. It had gray, thick doors and barred windows. The men were separated and put into one room, and the women and children into another. The room was big, nearly a hundred people in ours. There were rows of bunks with dark-green blankets neatly folded on each. We made our way to a bed next to the wall. Huddling together, we watched all the people speak so many different languages. Then, my sisters climbed up to the top bunk. My mother and I curled up on the bottom one. It was warm lying beside her body—it felt safe and good.

Even though we were on land, everything kept moving. I sensed my body still rising and falling. My head spun when I close my eyes. I drifted off into a hazy sleep. I startled to the sound of radiators banging, slamming, hissing steam. It was November 22, 1949, and the Nova Scotia nights were cold.

Suddenly, the sound of the steam filled the silence. Then, many of the women panicked and rushed from their beds toward the door. They screamed and pounded on the walls and the locked door. They shouted in Polish, German, and Yiddish while pointing at the steam hissing from the radiators.

I sat up in my bunk beside Ema, with Helle and Tiia in the bunk above us. My mother puts her arms around me, comforting me with gentle strokes. Only later, after learning about the Nazi death camps, did this scene make sense to me. The women were remembering the gas chambers.

Thus, our crossing ended. We arrived in North America, but no brass bands played and no one's outstretched hand greeted us. Instead, we were locked up with strangers afraid that we were being exterminated.

Finally, the customs officials let my father call his brother Ottomar in America. Ottomar explained to the officials that we had been rented a place in St. Catharines and that we would live on a farm owned by the Joll family, Estonians offering Ilmar work. This meant that our little Rakfeldt family would not become wards of the province.

The train station was very near Pier 21 in the harbor. We were allowed to board carrying our luggage with us. We also had a big wooden chest that was loaded separately.

The train moved slowly, making many stops as it rolled through Nova Scotia, New Brunswick, and Québec provinces before reaching Ontario. From the train window, the landscape seemed bleak—deep snow covered the fields and forests. Several times, the train stopped in the middle of nowhere. Workers had to dislodge the wet snow that had built up under the coaches. They then shoveled this snow out from underneath the train.

It seemed like the train stopped in every small village along the way. At one of these towns, my father and some other Estonians left the train to buy bread, cheese, and sausages. They were confident because they had an English phrasebook. In the shop, however, no one spoke English, only French. The clerk was rude and refused to serve them. The men learned quickly about the tensions between Francophone and English-speaking Canada. Fortunately, a boy in the shop's back room was brought out as a translator. We finally all feasted on bread, cheese, and sausage on the train.

In Toronto, the train made a very long stop. Peering from the train window, we marveled at the station's grandeur. It reminded me of the palatial train stations in London, with their high arching glass ceiling.

Finally, we began rolling slowly westward toward St. Catharines, Ontario. We arrived twenty-four hours later than scheduled. Freshly fallen snow covered the ground. Departing the train, I noticed the sweet aroma of fruitwood smoke and of cherry, apple, and peach rising from the chimneys of nearby houses.

Waiting for us when we got off the train was my uncle Ottomar, along with his whole family: his wife Florence and his three children, Harry, Johnnie, and Marie. His dark-green 1937 Chevy was parked right next to the tracks. Somehow, we managed to get everybody into his car—all ten of us, along with our suitcases. We drove along the four-lane highway until we turned into the Jolls' driveway, which led to a tiny, green-colored house next to the QEW. This would be our home in Canada.

Our first little rented house had only three rooms, a living room with a kitchen and two small bedrooms. There was also an attached woodshed in the back, where we stored the firewood. My sisters and I shared one of the bedrooms.

The big, brand-new home that had just been built next to us belonged to the Joll family, whose farm we lived on. The Joll family had three children of their own: Ines, Peeter, and Rita. Ines, who was the oldest, got married while we were there.

The Jolls also had a big St. Bernard, but he drooled a lot and was so big I was afraid of him. One day, he wandered into our house through an open door. Helle, Tiia, and I were so frightened that we ran into our bedroom. The harmless and gentle monster of a dog curiously walked through the curtain that separated the main room from ours. Frightened, we leaped onto the bed headboard while the puzzled dog looked up at us. He stood there, tongue hanging out, slobbering slightly, panting up at us with deep brown eyes, while we screamed for someone to help us. Ema finally heard our calls and ushered the dog out.

Our father initially struggled to find work. Quite literally, he beat the pavement until the soles of his shoes wore through, creating holes. He then donned galoshes over his shoes to cover the holes. He found employment on the fruit farms owned by Estonians—Misters Zirk, Neumann, and Kuhi, who had arrived before the war. Southern Ontario is known for its fruit-growing region, and St. Catharines is even called the Garden City. My mother worked in a snack bar attached to Simpson's gas station, which also housed a towing service and a car repair shop.

Our three-room house on the Jolls' farm stood next to the newly completed concrete four-lane divided highway constructed from Buffalo's Peace Bridge to Toronto—Queen Elizabeth Way, or the QEW. The entire length of the road was illuminated by ornate lampposts that featured, in elegant script, the letters "ER" for Elizabeth Regina. Standing beside the road, I watched the lampposts shrink until they finally vanished beyond the horizon.

Helle, Tiia, and I often ran across the four-lane divided roadway to visit Ema at a snack bar where she worked, and if we were lucky, we'd get a hot dog, candy, or some ice cream. We would watch for cars and wait for our chance to scamper quickly across. Once, Tiia's rubber boot got stuck in the wet, muddy median. She didn't stop but continued to run, mainly hopping on one foot. We later retrieved her boot, and all was well.

A highlight of our time in Canada was the New Year's Eve party in nearby Welland, Ontario. Even our trip to the party was memorable. Amazingly, Mr. Zirk, the local Estonian on whose farm Isa worked, managed to get us all, four adults plus three children, into the cab of his 1940 International Harvester pickup truck. Luckily, it was a short drive. The party was held in a large hall with a balcony and a big stage, upon which a dance band played tunes such as Glenn Miller's "In the Mood" and polkas and waltzes for the Estonian crowd. People did a lot of eating, drinking, singing, and dancing. I fell in with some young kids roughly my age. We played tag and hide-and-seek in the back of the big stage.

That night, I developed a real crush on a couple of very pretty Estonian girls who were dolled up in their frilly party dresses. That was the start of my special feelings for Estonian girls. At the party, we ran, chased, and caught each other, using the rows of tall, heavy, dark-red curtains to hide between and behind.

At last, I felt good being in Canada. And so, perhaps, leaving Sweden for Canada wasn't a bad idea after all.

Isa's day work often involved pruning grapevines and other farm laborer tasks. Mr. Kuhi was building a new house on his farm. He helped my father by making a deal with his plasterer, which stipulated that he would only hire him if he also gave work to my father as his helper.

This job did not last long. My father only worked with the plastering at five or six houses. He would stir the plaster mixture in a wheelbarrow so that the professional plasterers could do their work more quickly.

The plasterer, Maxim, was Russian. After the Russian Revolution and the end of World War I, many of Europe's borders changed dramatically. These changes left Maxim and his family in Poland instead of Russia. So, they came to Canada, where Maxim learned the craft of plastering and later became an independent contractor. Interestingly, his daughter happened to be born while they were traveling onboard the ship SS *Estonia*. And so, they named their daughter "Estonia."

My father's relationship with Maxim was very difficult and strained. Maxim was a staunch Russian nationalist who openly extolled Stalin's grand expansion of the Russian Empire as a massively enlarged Soviet Union after World War II.

I remember Maxim coming to dinner one night at our house, our tiny little place with only three rooms. A curtain hung in the doorway separating my and my sisters' bedroom from the main room, where Maxim and my parents sat at the dining table. As Maxim drank more vodka, the volume of his voice increased while my parents remained relatively quiet. Deep into the night, we heard them through the curtain. Maxim was a burly, stocky, muscular man who was typically animated and loud, and he became more so as the evening wore on.

Another problem with the plastering job was its inconsistency. During some weeks, there were only a couple of days of work, which resulted in a loss of income. So, during his free days, my father continued to search for work.

One place he visited was a small shop that made blocks and tackles. At that time, wooden blocks and tackles were still used on ships and for lifting heavy loads. Archimedes invented the block and tackle around 250 BCE. A block is a pulley, or set of pulleys, on an axle within a housing. A tackle is an assembly of blocks through which a rope can be run to lift loads.

My father asked the owner, Mr. Carlson, whether they had any jobs. He was told that they had nothing at that time. My father had seen the name Carlson painted in big letters on the outside wall of the building. As he turned to leave the office, he asked Mr. Carlson whether he was Swedish. Carlson said yes and added that his grandfather had come to Canada from Sweden. Immediately, my father spoke to him in Swedish. But it turned out that Carlson didn't speak Swedish, but his father still spoke the language. Carlson called his father into the office, after which the elder Carlson and my father exchanged pleasantries in Swedish. Following this exchange, they hired my father on the spot, telling him to come to work in the morning. His full-time job was making wooden blocks for the pulleys and tackles. For years, my mother had several thick, oval-shaped wooden cutting boards, half of a block, that my father brought home from work.

My father's use of Swedish provided leverage, like using a block and tackle to lift heavier weights or loads. A little bit of Swedish lifted my father into a job that would otherwise have been beyond reach.

We were on the final voyage of the famous ship *Aquitania* arriving in Halifax on November 22, 1949.

The *Aquitania* docked at Pier 21, November 1949.

This is the Carlson Canadian block company my father worked at in St. Catharines, Ontario.

Chapter 15

Finally, America: Isa's Dream, A Tree-Lined Allée

It was a beautiful Saturday afternoon on July 1, 1950, Canada Day, Canada's day of autonomy from the British Empire. We had lived in Canada since November 1949.

That day, we celebrated the holiday with the St. Catharines Estonian Evangelical Lutheran Church service and a summer picnic at Brock Memorial Park in Queenston Heights, Ontario. In the center of the park is a tall pillar with the statue of General Brock on top. Although Brock died during the battle, he is credited for winning against invading Americans during the War of 1812 at the battle of Queenston Heights.

General Brock monument in Queenston Heights Canadian National Park.

Following the short church service, there was a wonderful picnic with food and many treats for the kids. Vendors also sold goods and crafts. I remember seeing beautiful Estonian rings for sale. The Estonian coat of arms is enameled blue, black, and white with three golden lions embellished. I asked my mother if I could have one. She said I was too young with tiny fingers but would get one soon when my fingers got bigger.

The Estonian coat of arms ring,

It was a fun day with the kids running around playing hide-and-seek. We also had a beautiful view of the turbulent Niagara River deep below in the gorge.

During the event, Mr. Joll arrived in his truck and immediately approached my father with a quick stride and urgency. The Canadian Postal Service had just delivered a special delivery registered mail letter addressed to us from the United States naturalization and immigration administration.

My father opened the letter gently. As he read it, tears streamed down his cheeks—and it was very uncommon for him to show emotion. His hands shook as he handed the letter to my mother. My mother read it silently, and she began to tear up too.

Helle, Tiia, and I feared it might be bad news that we were being sent back to Sweden. My father looked down finally and said, "*Me läheme Ameerikasse.*" ("We are going to America.")

They had waited for this moment for six long years. Throughout all the difficulties, fears, and trials of our refugee lives, this had been their unending hope, our dream.

My parents told the others at the gathering, who congratulated and wished us well, adding they would miss us.

When we got home, we immediately called my uncle Ottomar across the border in Niagara County to plan our move to the States. This became one of the happiest days of our lives: We were going to America. Finally, America!

This last step of our journey involved crossing the U.S.–Canadian border. Except for a large wooden shipping crate delivered later, we packed everything we owned into two cars for the crossing into the United States. We used Ottomar's 1937 Chevy sedan and his sister-in-law Auntie Helen's Willys Jeep, a vintage woody station wagon.

On August 2, 1950, we drove the few miles from our house to the Lewiston–Queenston Bridge, an old suspension bridge with a wooden roadway that caused the boards to rattle as cars rolled over it. I sat scrunched up in the back of the Jeep on top of boxes and suitcases. This bridge, built in 1915, crossed the Niagara River at a narrow spot in the deep gorge. The suspension cables were attached directly to the gorge's rock face.

We went down a steep, winding, narrow road to the bridge. Isa and Onu Ottomar entered the small customs office building. It felt like forever before they finally came back out. They were both angry and frustrated. We had been refused entry into the United States, and we were prohibited from crossing the bridge into America. Isa had shown them our legitimate documents, but the officials would not let us pass through to the States. We then slowly drove back up the narrow, steep, winding road onto the QEW. But we were not done trying.

We drove west along the Niagara River until we arrived at the next bridge, the Whirlpool Rapids Bridge, a double-decked steel bridge with train tracks on the top and a roadway for cars below built in 1897. Isa and Onu Ottomar went into the customs office. And, once again, I sat for what felt like forever while squished into the back of the Jeep, squirming, trying to get more comfortable. Finally, Onu and Isa returned with smiles on their faces and good news. These customs officials would let us pass into the States. We were finally allowed to come to America.

After nearly a year in Canada, our place in the quota queue had arrived. My uncle Ottomar who helped us secure housing in St. Catharines took us into his home in America.

We arrived at Onu's small farmhouse on the Hess Road in Newfane, New York, only a few miles from the Niagara River.

Onu's wife Florence had made a big pot of *frikadellisupp* (an Estonian meatball soup), enough to feed all ten of us, five in our family and five in theirs. The farmhouse had one big bedroom on the second floor, with a smaller one on the first floor. Somehow, all ten of us lived there together for the first several weeks of our life in the States.

That fall, we rented a run-down, unpainted, ramshackle tenant house on Mr. Herr's large fruit farm. The house had no running water, indoor plumbing, or central heating. We warmed the house with a large cast-iron kitchen stove fueled by kerosene and a potbelly coal-burning stove in the living room. My father brought water in from a hand-pumped well.

My father pumping water for our needs.

The house had four rooms; the kitchen and living room were on the first floor and with two bedrooms upstairs. A stairway led up into the bedroom that I shared with my sisters. From there, a door led to our parents' bedroom. My sisters shared a full-size bed with a rounded brown steel headboard. I slept on a thin mattress placed upon wooden orange crates laid next to each other in the corner of the room. A chamber pot was placed in the middle of our room.

My mother picked fruit with the migrant workers on Mr. Herr's farm and other places, while my father worked the midnight shift at the Upson Wallboard Company in Lockport. Because we had no car, Isa walked more than a half mile to U.S. Route 104, the Ridge Road. He would take the public bus into Lockport, about fourteen miles away, and walked across the city from the downtown bus station to the factory. He worked the midnight shift from twelve to eight a.m. In the morning, he made this same trek back home.

During the day, Ema constantly shushed my sisters and me. Of course, we wanted to play and have fun, but we needed to be quiet not to wake up Isa, who needed his sleep. Isa learned English by voraciously reading books with the torn-off covers he brought home from the Upson factory. The company made four-by-eight-foot sheets of wallboard from pressed used paper from books, newspapers, and magazines. He also brought home comic books for us kids. He used these to bribe us into speaking Estonian. If we did, we got a comic book. His tactic worked as we all remained fluent in Estonian.

Ema worked picking cherries and other fruits with the migrant workers. Her pay was based on the number of baskets she filled. One day, two men arrived at our door. They were door-to-door Electrolux vacuum cleaner salesmen. They spent a long time at our house, demonstrating how great this Swedish vacuum was and explaining how it would make my mother's life easier. They were so persistent and persuasive that my mother ended up buying one. She spent all the money she had earned from weeks of picking cherries.

Very soon after they had left, she became overwhelmed by buyer's remorse. She feared what Isa would say when he learned about her extravagant purchase. And so, we helped her hide the cleaner under a pile of sheets and blankets stacked behind the couch in the corner of the living room. When Isa discovered her purchase, he was not upset, and everything turned out well. And the vacuum did indeed make all our lives easier.

Isa got a better job in Lockport at the Harrison Radiator Company, which is part of General Motors. This job came with good UAW union wages, health insurance, and retirement benefits. Later, Ema was able to get a job there too. With their two GM incomes, our lives improved. Isa bought Onu Ottomar's '37 Chevy. My parents could now drive to work, and we could go places as a family.

A couple of years later, my parents bought a shiny, light-green 1948 Dodge four-door sedan. Riding in this car felt like a luxury. I remember the day they brought it home. Late that night, I sat on the edge of my orange-crate bed, watching them from the window as Isa and Ema proudly washed and polished their new car. They were smiling and laughing, and I felt happy and proud too.

Our shiny new used 1948 Dodge with Tiia and me.

My parents' steady income eventually allowed us to purchase a thirty-two-acre farm on the nearby Dale Road in 1954 with the help of an old Estonian Great Lakes seaman who provided a private mortgage. We also bought a 1950 Ferguson tractor along with its many implements. Every day after work at Harrisons, my parents worked the farm. We all pitched in to do the many things that farm life required.

Our new house was set back from the road. A long driveway led to the house and was flanked on both sides by big maple trees. Isa told us that our tree-lined *allée* reminded him of Räägu Mõis (Räägu Manor) in Estonia, where they had lived before being forced to flee for their lives from the Russians, who swept across Estonia, killing, raping, and plundering. Even on the other side of the world, our parents retained a sense of the home they had left behind by living in a place with this tree-lined *allée*.

The tree-lined *allée* of Räägu Manor that motivated my parents to purchase this farm in Newfane.

Ottomar's 1937 Chevy Isa purchased from him with Tiia and part of our black dog Muri by our tenant house we rented.

Our Newfane house with the tree-lined *allée*.

Chapter 16

My Calling: A Life in Academia

In high school, I had a checkered academic record. I was not sure of myself and not slated for better things. But finally, an epiphany occurred. My English teacher, Mr. Vogt, asked me to present a lesson to the class. The topic was Shakespeare's use of iambic pentameter in his sonnets.

I worked hard to prepare, and I vividly remember presenting my lesson to the class. I stood straight and tall and with a full voice at the blackboard before my classmates, I boldly diagrammed Shakespeare's "When *I* / do *COUNT* / the *CLOCK* / that *TELLS* / the *TIME* . . ." to demonstrate the poetic rhythm. The experience transformed me. From that moment, I knew I wanted to be in academia.

Newfane High School provided a solid foundation. I had many outstanding teachers from whom I learned not only course content but also life lessons, among them Mr. Vogt, Mr. Kopeck, Mrs. Klock, Mr. Jay Haley, and Dr. Hunter.

In Mr. Kopeck's mechanical drawing class, we not only worked hard on our drawing projects, but he also shepherded us through discussions dealing with real-life issues. He taught us how to tie a full Windsor necktie knot. After I had mastered this skill, I felt like a real man.

Dr. Hunter, in addition to being an inspiring teacher and a great coach, took a group of us to Albright Knox Art Museum. There we spent the evening learning about and discussing the artworks.

During my senior year, the annual basketball game between the Newfane Faculty and the Varsity Club stands out as a meaningful memory. The faculty had great players and always won. In that game, as the first half ended, after a rebound, Fran Lampman, our star basketball and football player, got the ball. I ran to our basket, waving my hands as Fran brought the ball across midcourt. As the clock ran down, Fran shot from far away.

The ball clanged loudly off the rim and bounced high over to the side where tall, strong opposing team member John Chiavaro and I stood. We both jumped up and grabbed the ball, clinging to it as we dropped back down.

Somehow, I got the ball firmly into my hands. The instant my feet hit the floor, I leaped back up and took a shot. The ball swished through the hoop, nothing but net, right at the buzzer.

My teammates mobbed me, and the gym, packed with students, went wild with cheers. The Varsity Club took its first and only lead by one point. Even though we lost the game, this moment remains a warm and fond memory of my Newfane High School years.

Despite such successes, I had a chip on my shoulder. My academic record was checkered. I did well when I applied myself but not when I didn't. This was my way of rebelling, of thumbing my nose at the system, showing them that I wasn't beholden to anyone.

But when my mother and I met with a guidance counselor, he told me, "You are not college material." My mother looked stunned. On our drive home, tears streamed down her face. Lying on the corner of my desk at home were piles of college applications. Now, there seemed no purpose in submitting them.

Not long after, while walking past the counseling office, I saw the secretary waving to me. She asked if I had signed up to take the New York State Regents Scholarship Exam. A few weeks later, I spent a Friday in the little gymnasium with rows of others taking the all-day test. When the scholarship winners were announced in homeroom, I was shocked to hear my name. Others stared at me in bewildered disbelief. That night, I sent my application into Geneseo and got accepted.

At freshman orientation, my college classmates and I assembled in Wadsworth Hall. The dean stood on stage and told us to look to the left and the right of us. He ominously added that by the end of that school year, only one of us would still be a student. This admonition seared through my heart. The words "You are not college material" still haunted me.

But Dr. John O. Hunter's wise words guided me: "Organization is the key to success." My organizing strategy was to spread out my books and papers in a carrel up behind the stacks in the library. Promptly at five p.m., I'd cross the quad to the cafeteria to be first in line. I would wolf down my dinner and hurry back to the library, where I often studied until I heard the chimes from the clock tower carillon at eleven p.m., when the library closed.

I ended up doing remarkably well. I got two master's degrees, a PhD, and a postdoctoral fellowship, a research scientist position, a clinical position at Yale University, and a professorship at Southern Connecticut's graduate school.

My high school graduation photograph (1964).

My first master's degree graduation with my parents, Arnold, and Heli (1972).

Chapter 17

At Last, the Homeland of My Heart

Summer 1974, Estonia

My first trip on the ferry from Helsinki to Tallinn in 1974 lasted about four hours. As we neared land, I stood in the front of the upper deck, straining to catch my first glimpse of Tallinn. It was powerfully gripping when, on the gray horizon, towers and smokestacks began to emerge. I trembled as I tried to hold my camera still while shooting pictures of the looming city panorama. I recognized St. Olaf's Church, built in the twelfth century. At one time, it may have been the tallest building in the world. During the Soviet occupation the KGB used the spire as a radio tower and surveillance point.

Slightly to the left was the Hotel Viru, Estonia's first skyscraper, built two years earlier by a Finnish company with primarily Finnish labor and materials. Its purpose was to showcase the Soviet Intourist agency. At the time, the hotel was the only place tourists were allowed to stay in Tallinn. The Soviet secret police had a secret unmarked top floor, the twenty-third, above the "top floor" restaurant. The KGB used this as a spy base with various electronic listening and monitoring devices. It was an open secret that the secret police used this hotel to keep track of foreign guests and monitor any locals with whom they interacted.

Arriving in Estonia for the first time with the skyline of Tallinn growing larger.

After docking, Russian officials came on board to check our documents. Again, at the bottom of the stairs on the dock departing the ship, our documents were rechecked, and long scrutinizing stares were focused on each passenger who had descended the narrow staircase. Carrying my bulging backpack, I walked into the customs building, where I stood in a long line waiting to provide my documents again and to have my person and backpack rummaged thoroughly by Russian officers who did not speak Estonian and almost no English.

The Viru Intourist Hotel in the 1970s.

We were met immediately by Intourist personnel, who were not a friendly group. They demanded that we give them our passports (which they kept until we left ten days later) before allowing us to board the bus for the Hotel Viru, only a short drive away. At least our room in the two-year-old building was modern and clean, with a large window overlooking the city. My roommate was Valdar Oinas, a member of our MÜ group. He was a quiet, intelligent, and genuinely nice person. He told me to be careful because everything we said was probably being listened to. I was overwhelmed by a mixture of joy and anguish. It was a joy to be there, but now I faced the agony of the horrific Russian occupation and oppression.

To my surprise, I saw Silja, the woman I'd met in Finland, in the hotel lobby. She told me to get ready to go quickly because she and her friends were taking me to dinner. The next thing I knew, I was riding to the Saku collective farm near Tallinn in their car. At the city border stood a tall structure with a gigantic projector light and a boom barrier bar that could be pivoted up or down to block vehicles from passing through this controlled checkpoint that monitored those who came and left Tallinn. We were allowed to drive straight through past the armed soldiers.

The main hall of the collective farm had a big restaurant with a live band performing on a low stage for patrons to dance and listen. The food was acceptable. The beer was brewed right at the farm and was somewhat murky. Our friendly conversation flowed freely with Silja, Valeri, and his girlfriend. All at once, Silja looked serious. Pointing discreetly with her finger, her hand still lying on the table, she said quietly that a man at a nearby table was KGB. Of course, I started to turn to look, but she whispered sharply for me not to.

A wet blanket had been thrown onto my good feelings. Soon after this, we left the restaurant. Valeri dropped me off at the hotel. At the door, I was met by uniformed men who asked who I was, which room I was staying in at the hotel, and for me to show them the pass I had been given. When I arrived at my floor, two middle-aged women sat at a table near the elevators and noted my arrival into a large ledger.

Our room was empty; my roommate wasn't there. I lay on the bed with conflicting thoughts and emotions swirling. *Who really is Silja? How does she have access to this tightly controlled hotel? Why has she taken such an interest in me?* I never really was able to answer any of these questions.

The Intourist people had a full itinerary and expected everyone to always stay with the group. We had lectures with graphs depicting the success of their Soviet five-year plans. All the indicators pointed upward toward progress. We were taken to showcase venues where we were wined, dined, and treated like royalty.

We first visited the Kirovi Kolhoos, a fishing collective on the Viimsi peninsula near Tallinn. It was built in 1950 and was named after Sergei Kirov, an early Russian Bolshevik, who was a leading revolutionary figure but was murdered in 1934 by Stalin as part of his great purges.

The collective was a top Estonian showcase during the 1970s and 1980s, with its stylish buildings, employee rewards, and generous allotments for members. It was later described as a surreal bubble of comfort and affluence in occupied Estonia, where poverty, fear, and despair prevailed. This was always the first stop for every Intourist-led trip for foreigners. We spent several hours of our first day there drinking and eating while listening to propaganda.

We visited several showcase collectives, such as the Yuri Gagarin collective pig farm named after the famed Russian cosmonaut. Intourist tried to keep us together through all their showcase sites while invariably extolling the clear superiority of Communism over Western decadence and decay.

Despite this regimentation, absenteeism among the MÜ group increased. Unlike typical foreign tourist groups, we all spoke Estonian fluently, and most had friends and family living here.

After my first MÜ experience, I had devoted myself to improving my Estonian language skills; I spoke it whenever I visited home with my parents and their friends. Estonian is a phonetic language, so I would read it out loud, sounding out the words. Hearing the words led to understanding what I read with the help of an Estonian–English dictionary. The good news was that when I was in Estonia, locals did not even realize I was from America.

The inability to herd our group drove our Intourist leader to distraction. She had several emotional meltdowns and was on the verge of a complete breakdown. Looking back, I realize she was probably frightened for her well-being, given her taskmasters.

Silja and Valeri asked if I would like to visit Pärnu, a seaside resort in the south. Instead, I told them I wanted to see my parents' home, Räägu Manor. And so, despite all the Soviet warnings and my parents' trepidation, I played hooky from the Intourist official itinerary, and we set out for Räägu on the west coast near the city of Haapsalu.

Once again, we passed the checkpoint and drove out of Tallinn along Paldiski Road without being stopped. Valeri was not familiar with the route. He missed our turn and continued into a restricted zone nearing Paldiski, a highly guarded Russian nuclear submarine base.

Big signs warned drivers to stop immediately. Valeri panicked and turned around. We found the proper turn-off and headed in the right direction along the Keila–Haapsalu Road. There was virtually no traffic, which was true throughout Estonia then.

A couple of slow-moving farm trucks in front of us began slowing down even more to a walker's pace. Soon, big buildings and huge stone mounds appeared on the left-hand side, surrounded by a high fence topped with barbed wire. On the right were more buildings and barracks. This was a prison named Rummu.

Built in 1938, it had wooden structures for a guard post, two barracks, and a factory for the stone quarry workers. During the Soviet occupation, it became a much larger slave-labor prison for political prisoners and criminals, who lived and worked under harsh conditions and worked at the stone quarry.

Our car was barely moving. Suddenly, about six or seven Russian soldiers were walking in a close formation beside the car window on my side. They had automatic weapons on their backs. They were right next to me, only three feet away. I looked like a Westerner with a Nikon camera in my lap. I slumped forward, dropping my head, pretending to be asleep. My heart pounded, sweat beads formed on my forehead, and my breathing shallowed. Was it over? Would we go to jail? Were we all getting arrested? Would I be charged as a Western spy, caught red-handed with a fancy camera next to a Soviet prison camp, and end up in one myself?

But the soldiers had better things to do. We passed through and drove along the narrow, winding road past road signs with names familiar to me from my parents' stories, such as Risti and Palivere. I felt the excitement building as we neared my parents' former home. It was like a dream. It was hard to believe I was actually here.

Soon, we arrived at Linnamäe, my parents' home village. I knew that Räägu Manor was ahead toward the west. We passed an open field with a stand of trees at the end. A narrow road turned off, and I saw a stone storage building beside it. We passed tall old oak trees with a footpath leading to a large building deep within the stand of trees.

I told Valeri, "I think this is it. This is Räägu." I pointed down the path. At the first house, we turned left into its driveway. Valeri got out, knocked on the door, and asked where Räägu Manor was.

The man standing in the doorway pointed back to that tall stand of oak trees. I was right. I had recognized Räägu based on all the stories I had heard about it while growing up.

My heart pounded. I was here. I was living a dream.

We drove back toward the manor, turned into the narrow road, and passed the stone storage shed. At the fork in the road, we turned left toward the back of the manor house. A circular driveway passed several outbuildings and a barn. There was a wooden shed-like shelter my uncle Arnold had built to cover the well. It had a hand crank for lowering a bucket into the well and bringing it back up filled with water. I recall Onu Arnold describing building this structure to protect the well and keep the water clean.

Because I was there illegally, I didn't dare talk to anyone. We parked and walked around to the front of the manor by the east end. This was where my parents' apartment had been and where my sisters had lived when they were small. I wished I could have seen the inside, but that would have been too dangerous. This was the tree-lined *allée* leading to the main road that had inspired my parents to buy our house in Newfane.

About halfway out toward the road, next to the footpath, a stone maker read, "Great Homeland War—Four Fallen Unknown Soviet Soldiers." Later, I learned from the family who lived upstairs in the manor that these soldiers were not unknown but bivouacked troops in the manor's park who had died from consuming a large amount of bad homebrewed moonshine. They were buried there in the park with honors as heroes of the "Great Homeland War," as Russians refer to WWII.

As I walked back toward the manor, a man stood on the front porch and repeatedly yelled something in Russian at me. I froze.

It's over, I thought. *I'm caught.* Valeri stood behind me and whispered to take the man's picture, which I did. He smiled and waved. I waved back, grinning. He turned and went back indoors.

I imagined how Räägu looked in the 1930s when my family lived there. In the photo, you can see an open staircase facing forward. My mother told me how one of their friends, Salum, once rode his big white horse up the stairs into the center ballroom during a party, rode around the hall once, and galloped his steed back out the door and down the front stairs.

Walking along, I wondered under which big oak trees Isa had buried their documents and photos. I wished I knew. My parents had also left flax fibers soaking in the river that flowed through the park, planning to later transform these into linen that could be woven into fabric for clothing. The stream was now merely a tiny ditch after Russian "land improvement" projects had drained huge areas around it to create more tillable land, which destroyed the whole region's ecology.

We drove to the big flour mill where my father and uncle had spent days, weeks, months, and years working to pay off their mortgage and provide for their growing families. Farmers from near and far brought their grain to be milled into flour there. My uncle and father purchased the bankrupt mill, the manor, and more than forty hectares of land in 1934. Father's name could not be on the deed because he was still too young. Only six years later, in 1940, they had paid their debt in full, through hard work and determination. But the first Soviet occupation in the same year nationalized Räägu. My family lost everything for no compensation. Nevertheless, they were still allowed to stay there. My parents later fled to the woods, until the Nazi occupation drove the

Russians out during the summer of 1941. In 1942, Onu Arnold requested that the manor be returned to them, which was granted, but in September 1944, he and my father and their families left everything behind when they fled for their lives as the brutal Soviet onslaught swept through once again during the second Soviet occupation.

I had heard so much about their work in the gristmill. As we approached, I saw the big three-story limestone structure appear.

I climbed up the stairs to the third floor and saw giant milling machines that my father, uncle, and a hired worker had worked with their hands. A spiritual connection to them swept through me as I slid my fingers over these artifacts. Farmers brought grain loads, pulling wagons under the sack hoist or winch over the front entrance, as shown in the photo. It consisted of a drum and rope manually turned to hoist the grain bags up to the third floor. The grain was then poured into the milling machines, which processed it into flour as it fell by force of gravity through the grinding millstones to the first floor. The flour was loaded back onto the farmer's wagon and taken away. My father described how long lines of horse-drawn wagons and trucks often waited deep into the night during the height of the season. They constantly worked long days, fifteen or more hours, to mill all the grain from as far away as nearby Vormsi Island.

The mill was initially built in the 1600s and was powered by water from the river that flowed past it then. Rudolf Krupp, from whom they bought it, had powered the mill with electricity until he went bankrupt. The worldwide economic crisis of the early 1930s led to extremely high energy costs, which meant the mill operated at a loss. The first thing my father and uncle did was to replace the power that turned the millstones with a diesel engine. Cheap diesel fuel allowed them to earn a profit and pay off their debt.

I stepped into the wooden shed that housed their motor and saw the rusted engine they had personally installed. Again, I sensed a connection with them as I touched the remains of this machinery. This connection to their strength evoked a deep bond with my heritage, parents, and ancestors. They prevailed through extremely harsh times while retaining human dignity, decency, humor, love, compassion, and zest for living.

During the drive back to Tallinn, my thoughts remained with having touched with my own hands the machines my father and Uncle Arnold had worked with their own hands. Years later, in 1995, I had an episode of a deep connection to my father's and uncle Arnold's hands. It occurred the night of my first class dealing with psychopathology right after I started my new job as a professor in the graduate program of Southern Connecticut State University.

While setting up my new office I hung the last plaque in my new office. The nail I placed through the hook's eye slipped as I hit it with the hammer. Pain shot through my finger into my hand. It throbbed. I sucked it. The tip turned blue.

I stared at my hand. My mind turned to my Uncle Arnold's place on Lake Ontario. Flood waters once threatened his home, boathouse, and sauna. We nailed plywood to the walls, feverishly filled sandbags, and piled them against the buildings. Arnold stood in the water, hammer in hand, tacking boards to his house. I stood above him, handing him tools. My godfather was in his seventies by then. His hands were strong, skilled, gnarled, and knobby.

The flood at Arnold's home by Lake Ontario, 1970s.

Now, in my office, I stared at my throbbing hand. A blue blood blister filled the tip of my index finger. I imagined Arnold and my father in their mill in Estonia, their hands white with freshly milled flour, grasping the cogs, straining to turn the giant wooden wheel, and slowly lifting the bags of grain from the ground to the third floor.

In my mind's eye, I saw my father's hands, his mangled fingers that he'd caught in a textile factory machine when we lived in Sweden. His fingernails grew at odd angles. He cut them using big red rounded wire cutters. His hands had worked as a miller and a plasterer in textile, paper, and automobile factories, not to mention the years of farm work. His hands were firm and solid. As a kid, I tried to test my strength against his. I'd push with all my might to move his hands. He'd hold firm. While swimming in our pond, I'd try to push him under. He was a rock. He'd hold me up with one outstretched hand—his mangled, gnarled, perfect hand.

At the end of that amazing day, we drove back to Tallinn along the newer Route 9 highway (Ääsmäe–Haapsalu–Rohuküla Road) so we'd avoid the Soviet prison and getting lost and wandering into a restricted zone again. I had purchased a bottle of Georgian Cognac as a thank-you gift to share with the others for taking me to Räägu.

We then went to Valeri's parents' garden cottage near the Tallinn airport. It was among many similar small cabins surrounded by garden plots. His parents lived in a Soviet-style cement five-story apartment building on the busy Karl Marx Boulevard, which offered no secure garden space. Those lucky or well-connected enough could get a small plot under the airport's flight path to grow vegetables. Such plots significantly improved life because good quality produce was often unavailable and so was impossible to buy at the store.

My cousin's daughter once worked in a small food store. She was much sought after by people who always wanted to befriend her—acquaintances are to Communism what money is to capitalism. With trusted contacts, people could surreptitiously barter or buy things under the table that were unavailable on store shelves. In this way, corruption became a usual way of life for everyone across the spectrum, young and old, Communist Party members and elites and ordinary people.

Valeri built a fire in the big kitchen stove with its chimney passing through a *soemüür* (literally "warm wall") where the smoke and heat from the kitchen stove and oven are captured in the thick masonry wall, stored, and then radiated out into the main room.

This works by having the smoke pass through baffles inside the brick wall of the chimney. During the summer, the chimney can be opened directly to the sky by removing a damper, so the house does not overheat. This is a very efficient and common architectural feature of homes throughout Estonia. Even on this cool summer night, the *soemüür* created a warm and cozy space to enjoy dinner, a drink, and conversation.

When I returned to the hotel, once again, I was confronted by uniformed men. On my hotel floor, the women recorded my arrival into their ledger.

The next day, on my own but constantly shadowed by my own special KGB officer, I explored Tallinn's old town near the hotel. It dates to the eleven hundreds and is like a fairy-tale town with narrow cobblestone streets, a castle fortress perched high on a hill surrounded by walls, and beautiful towers and gates.

Later, I took a bus to the ruins of the Pirita Convent or cloister, about eight kilometers away. Surprisingly, the KGB officer was there too. The Pirita ruins are magnificent. The convent was built in 1407 by the Bridgettine Order, a Catholic religious order founded by Saint Bridget of Sweden. Sadly, the cloister was brutally attacked and destroyed by the Russian army in 1575, along with the nearby houses and villages.

In shops and public places, I heard the official radio constantly beaming programs and news with a decidedly Soviet propaganda slant. Unlike typical radios, these had no on and off switch. The sound of government propaganda was ubiquitous, ever-present.

This was the time of drought in Ukraine, and the Soviets were forced to purchase grain from the United States. Some in Congress felt the price was too low and referred to the deal as the "great grain robbery." Instead of reporting this truth, the Soviet news kept glamorizing the "heroes of the socialist people" with images of collective farm workers harvesting record crops of grain.

Later, while visiting my cousin's family, I watched the evening news show clips of workers being awarded the "Lenin medal" by local Communist Party officials while standing next to their tractors and combines in wheat fields. The clips would begin and end with wheat flowing freely into big bins. When I told my relatives that this was a lie and that the Russians were buying grain from the West because of a bad harvest in Ukraine, they just stared at me in disbelief.

Tallinn is a fairy-tale city with walls, towers, turrets, and a hilltop fortress.

Everywhere I walked throughout the old town, I saw a man carrying a leather briefcase following me. He was the KGB agent assigned to watch and report all my activities. I was annoyed and purposely took pictures of him. Although this may have been provocative, I wanted a record of what was happening to me. He didn't seem to mind my camera pointed at him. Of course, being followed like this was unnerving and filled me with anger, fear, and anxiety. Being followed tarnished my experience of old Tallinn and Pirita and, to some extent, tainted my first trip to Estonia, my odyssey, my parents' homeland, in search of my identity and heritage.

My KGB agent was following me in the Tallinn old town.

My KGB agent at the ruins of the Pirita Cloister.

My KGB agent at the outside of the ruins of the Pirita Cloister.

As part of the Intourist activities, we were bussed to Pärnu, the summer resort town in southwest Estonia. The bus roof leaked when it rained, so people opened their umbrellas inside to stay dry. We swam and enjoyed the wonderful sandy beach at Pärnu. The city is a summer resort, spa, and recreation destination.

Pärnu has been inhabited since the Stone Age and is one of the five members of the Hanseatic League, which emerged in the twelfth century as a coalition of merchant guilds in Northern and Western Europe. Its goal was to promote trade and serve as a mutual defense alliance. Estonia has five Hanseatic cities: Tallinn, Pärnu, Tartu, Viljandi, and Narva. This explains Estonian culture as embodying Western culture, customs, and values.

From there, we went to Viljandi, east of Pärnu. Viljandi is a charming town with historic architecture, many cultural events, and natural beauty overlooking a lake and valley. Viljandi has medieval ruins of a fortress, old churches, and a well-preserved old town district. We stayed overnight at a charming old hotel. Our Intourist guide had a major meltdown when we all went out independently across the area without her permission and supervision.

The next day, we went to Tartu, the country's second-largest city, with a long, rich history dating back over a thousand years. The University of Tartu was founded in 1632, making it one of the oldest in Northern Europe. For Estonians Tartu is their intellectual and spiritual center. We toured the city and the university but were carefully herded back onto the bus because Tartu was a restricted zone due to a Soviet air base nearby.

The Russian man yelled at me. After I took his photo, he went back into the building.

My father and Arnold used this wheel to wench the bags of grain to the third floor.

Silje and Valeri in front of the mill.

The local school art teacher painted this mural on the wall of what was the ballroom, depicting the life at Räägu when the Rakfeldts lived there in the 1930s.

Räägu during the 1930s when my family lived there. Notice the open front facing stairs and columns.

Valeri is standing next to the diesel motor house my father and Arnold installed.

The Räägu gristmill in 1974 when I first saw it.

I climbed the stairs to the third floor of the flour mill.

Arnold described building this shed for the well when I was young. I have always had an image of it, and it looks much like I had imagined.

A photo in the back of Räägu of Arnold's wife, Hilda, and their daughters, Milvi and Leili.

Chapter 18

My Newfound Family United in Song

Even though my parents hadn't objected to my coming to Estonia, they were concerned that my visit might harm our relatives. They even arranged for me to receive their hand-delivered letter through a group member from Toronto during the trip, strongly reminding me not to contact relatives and to stay only with the MÜ group. I tried to follow their wishes, but it turned out my family in Estonia had other plans.

Naadi, a relative of mine from Cleveland, visited Estonia earlier that year and told my family there that I would be coming with the MÜ group in August after our conference ended in Finland in 1974. Naadi's great-grandfather and my great-grandmother were brother and sister, and Naadi's uncle married my aunt, Ida, my mother's sister. So, we also shared common cousins, Tamme Meeta and Helvi.

My mother's brother, Onu Volli, also listened to the Voice of America through the screeching and crackling of the Soviet scrambled broadcasts and learned precisely when I would arrive. He hung around the heavily guarded Intourist hotel several times, hoping to find me. In addition, Naadi's mother, Miia, contacted the hotel and left a message for me to call her back.

When I received the message, anguish flooded through me. While I badly wanted to meet them and they were so nearby, I still wanted to be true to my promise and respect my parents' wishes. My anxiety and tension rose, and my stomach churned. Exhilaration and sadness entwined in my chest. Pacing around my hotel room, I stopped to gasp fresh air from the window. I desperately wanted to meet family, but without breaking my promise to my parents.

Laying back on the bed with my legs propped up, I steeled myself. I reasoned, perhaps justified, that if I were careful not to break any of the Soviet-imposed rules, it could turn out all right. I had met Miia a few years earlier when she had somehow gotten permission to visit family in America. Finally, after settling myself, I was emboldened to return Miia's call. I said I could meet them at her place.

Miia told me to take tramcar Number 4 from in front of the hotel. This tram runs along Pärnu Road to the Tondi stop, which is very near her home, 26 Matrossovi Street.

After I had recovered enough to change my clothes and freshen up, I walked across Pärnu Road to the flower vendors' stands. I bought a beautiful bouquet. Then, carefully carrying the bouquet upside down, I walked back to the tram stop, as people there did.

My tension increased as I waited for the Number 4 tram. Never having faced circumstances like meeting close blood relatives for the first time in Estonia, behind the Iron Curtain, I felt excited and anxious. I rationalized that because I did not initiate the contact, I was less culpable for defying my parents' wishes. I vowed that I would not do anything to jeopardize them. I would follow the Intourist rules to the letter, like not leaving Tallinn with them to go anywhere else.

I boarded the tram, clipped my ticket in the machine, and found a seat, my mind racing with thoughts. What if someone there was a Marxist? What if one of them turned out to be a KGB informant? Would my less-than-perfect Estonian language skills create a barrier between us? I had long hair and a beard. I feared they would judge me negatively and reject me at first sight. My heart pounded. My breath came in shallow gasps. I studied the street signs, worried I would miss my stop. A mix of excitement, anxiety, and dread flowed through me. This was more than just a short tram ride; it was a bridge to new relationships, a deeper understanding of my heritage, and the culmination of hearing countless stories passed down to me through the years.

Excitement crackled around my head like static electricity. I imagined the warm embraces from relatives I had only seen in faded photographs and heard about during family gatherings. What would they be like? Would I see traces of myself in them? The anticipation of finally putting faces to names ignited a spark of joy within me.

Yet, intertwined with my excitement was a thick thread of anxiety. Would I fit in with my family? What if our shared blood did not guarantee shared values, hopes, dreams, or interests? The fear of long awkward silences loomed over me like a dark storm cloud. It was a daunting thought to meet people who held pieces of my identity yet were total strangers.

And then, there was the dread—a faint but persistent whisper in the back of my mind. What if my expectations didn't match reality? What if the connections I longed to build fell flat or revealed a family history darker than I could have imagined? The weight of uncertainty pressed heavily on me.

I got off where Matrossovi Street forks off to the right from Pärnu Road. I looked for and quickly found the house. I was ready to face whatever lay ahead, embrace the unknown, and discover my family's roots. Exhilaration coursed through me once more. I was about to embark on a significant chapter of my life, and no matter what happened, I was prepared to embrace every moment of it.

The house was a 1930s Estonian apartment building with nine apartments above the basement level, where they sold pastries from their bakery. Like so many buildings in Tallinn, it badly needed repair and fresh paint. A central hallway with a staircase led up to the apartment doors. My family lived on the first floor on the left side.

Miia and Willem greeted me warmly, smiling and shaking my hand, happy to see me, and offered me coffee and sweet pastries. Miia's husband was originally named Willem Heeringas ("herring"). They changed their family name to Saluste because kids made fun of their daughter Naadi's name, calling her "*kala*" ("the fish").

They described how this house had been their home before the war. They had owned a bakery and were solidly middle class, even owning a Buick automobile. They told me they had owned the bakery building just behind their house and had a storefront selling baked goods on the lower level. After the Russian occupation in 1940, they lost their bakery. The Russians arrested Willem on fabricated charges. In a quick show trial, he was sentenced to years of prison. They charged him with being a black marketeer. But his only "crime" was being a modestly successful bakery owner. Having a Buick parked in his garage compounded his criminality.

Russians took the family's business and the building with the nine apartments and imprisoned Willem. After serving his sentence, Willem could not return to his home in Tallinn for several years. A woman named Mia, who was a relative, moved into their shared space.

With the help of a Communist friend, they were permitted to move back into the pantry area of their old apartment building. Now his bakery and his Buick were gone. I was shocked to hear all of this. My heart ached while having coffee and sweet pastries with such kind, warm, humble people.

Soon, other relatives arrived as word got out that I was at Miia's. Miia told me that many others would be coming. Soon, Tamme Meeta arrived, as did Helvi, Vääna Meeta, and Onu Volli.

Volli was my mother's big brother, with whom she had a close relationship. Ema told me how Volli always looked out for her and was always ready to help her in any way that he could. Sadly, Volli had been working at his job with the railroad, so Ema could not see him to say goodbye before they escaped. He was a big man, tall and robust, with a full head of blond hair. He grasped my hand firmly with his railroad man's grip and looked deeply into my eyes.

Tears formed in his blue eyes. He said repeatedly, "*Jaak, sa oled nii väga Miralda moodi.*" ("You look so much like Miralda.") I've been told that all my life—that I have my mother's green eyes, blond hair, and high cheekbones. Looking up into Volli's eyes almost brought a swelling of tears for me too, but I pushed them back down.

Everyone was warm and welcoming. We talked, ate, drank, and sang Estonian songs while Meeta's husband Rein played the guitar. They were amazed and glad that I knew the words too.

They wanted to hear about our life in America, but I was much more interested in hearing about their extraordinary lives. My mother's younger sister, Väänа Meeta, invited me to dinner at her home. They also wanted to take me to Aru Talu, their childhood home in coastal western Estonia, where they planned to have a fancy dinner for me with family. But I told them I could not go there with them. Meeta's face turned downward with disappointment and perhaps hurt, which saddened me. I hadn't wanted this. I explained that I would love to see Aru Talu, but it would be too dangerous for them. I didn't want to make any trouble for them, as I had promised my parents.

The truth was that a couple of days earlier, I had secretly been very near Aru Talu (about two miles away) when Silja and Valeri took me to Räägu Manor, where my parents had lived before escaping. I had risked going with them because they were not family and would not be as vulnerable. I was mindful of my parents' concerns not to jeopardize our family.

I did go to Meeta's for dinner near Tallinn. It was powerfully gratifying to sit at the table that belonged to my parents in Räägu and that Meeta had taken home after my parents fled and before the Russians came.

Meeta described how the Russians feared the big bull at Räägu named Tõnu as he stood, staring at them, snorting, and pawing the ground with his hoof. So, they shot him from a safe distance while he was chained to a post. As I listened to Meeta describe this, an image of how my family could have faced the bull Tõnu's fate at the hands of the Russians burst into my mind.

It was terrific meeting all these family members. My mother's family was musically talented, singing and playing instruments like the guitar, mandolin, and harmonica. We talked, ate, and sang together. Even though I was painfully aware of my language shortcomings, they praised me for how well I spoke Estonian. They were even more astonished that I knew the lyrics to the old Estonian songs we sang.

I knew these songs because while growing up, I spent so much time with my parents and their friends at parties filled with music. These songs became an essential part of who I am. This strong legacy of songs maintained the Estonian identity. The power of choral singing and song festivals has maintained Estonian identity even in the face of powerful Russification pressures and through all the terror, tumult, and trauma of centuries of foreign occupation.

Once back at my hotel, that night I lived a dream, singing old familiar songs with my newfound family.

Viljandi paadimees	Viljandi Boatman
Käe ulatab noor paadimees nii lahkelt neiule, kes aralt seisab tema ees, et sõita üle vee. Ta kaela neiu langeb siis ja kingib suudluse. Silm särab rõõmupisarais, arm tungib südame.	Young boatman offers his hand, So kindly to the maiden, Who stands shyly, and grand, To cross the lake, unladen. Then she embraces him with bliss, And gifts him a sweet kiss. Her eyes shine with tears of joy. Love invades their hearts, no ploy.

We sat at the table they had removed from my parents' place in Räägu. I felt a connection to the table and to my newfound family, singing and enjoying time together.

Chapter 19

My Father's Life as an "Outlaw," a "Lindprii"

When the Nazi–Soviet Pact, known as the Molotov–Ribbentrop Treaty, was signed on August 23, 1939, the Nazis took full advantage of this to invade Poland in September. The Russians, meanwhile, forced conditions upon the Baltics that amounted to an invasion of them under the veneer of a mutual defense agreement that was forced upon them, sending thousands of troops to the bases there. The rest of the world was unprepared and did little to protest these invasions. Then, to legitimize their illegal takeover, the Soviets staged a referendum in which the population ostensibly voted to join the Soviet Union, but with thousands of Russian occupation soldiers stuffing the ballot boxes. With that sham referendum, the Soviets created a puppet government. Estonia was fully annexed into the Soviet Union by August 1940.

Resistance was quelled brutally. They began to execute military men and political leaders and sent business owners and wealthy farmers to the gulags. Eventually, the arrests and deportations of intellectuals, property owners, and military professionals culminated in mass arrests throughout Estonia in June 1941. No one knew where they would strike next.

July 3, 1941

Ilmar had been warned. The clerk in the town hall, Ilmar's brother-in-law August "Kutt" Allmäe, had told him the KGB had been searching through town records. Ilmar's name was third from the top on the list of those to be taken away. Why? No one could say.

There was no clear reason as to how names got onto these lists. Ilmar's and Kutt's names were listed, perhaps, because they had been in the Estonian Army Reserve and belonged to the Defensive Alliance Organization (the National Guard).

On the evening of July 3, 1941, Kutt told Ilmar and two of his friends, Ago and Herbert, to meet the town supervisor (Kutt's boss) at the town hall. They would be violating the nighttime movement curfew that the Soviet Narodnyy Komissariat Vnutrennikh Del (NKVD) forces had imposed. But Ago's radio and hunting rifles, which had been collected by the Soviets, were locked in a box in the town's jail cell. Although the supervisor had been appointed by the Russian occupation authorities, he wasn't a Communist. At their meeting, he gave Ago's property back to him—the radio and the guns. He then put bricks into the lockbox so that it would appear as though the items were still there and locked them back into the jail cell.

Before people of the town began to wake up, the men had to return to the woods where they had been hiding since the mass deportations of June 13 and 14. But the midsummer days were long, while the nights were short. The men hardly noticed how much time was passing. At about four in the morning, in the distance they heard the sound of a truck coming from the Haapsalu to the west. It stopped at the crossroads in Linnamäe, then things were quiet again.

Ilmar went to get his bicycle from in front of the building. But, before he could open the outside door, he saw four NKVD soldiers approaching the town hall through a side window. He whispered loudly to the others that strangers were coming. Ago and Herbert climbed through the building's back windows. The town supervisor and Ilmar ran out of the side door.

About four hundred feet from the back of the house was an old apple orchard, and just beyond this was a rye field. With a little slouching and bending, the four men could hide in the tall rye stalks; luckily, the morning was so misty and foggy that they were barely visible. The supervisor went home, and Ago and Herbert went to conceal their rifles. Ilmar agreed to meet them later in a neighboring farmer's pasture.

When the NKVD approached the town hall, Kutt Allmäe came to the door and acted like he had been sleeping. It became clear that this was the day for the deportation of the people from the township, particularly men who had been members of the Kaitse Liit (the National Guard). Kutt was arrested on the spot.

Ilmar was still in the rye field when the township's courier went past on his way to the supervisor's house, but he didn't trust him enough to ask what was going on. The courier then passed him again on his way back to the town hall. All the while, Ilmar hid in the shadows. But he was worried about his bicycle, which he really needed to get around.

Ilmar made his way toward the front of the building to see who was coming or going. The early morning mist and fog were still dense, so he could not see the front doorway very clearly. But the nickel-chrome of his Swedish bike glittered even in the dim light. He had to lie down because there were only a few low shrubs to hide behind. He watched and waited anxiously, afraid to get his bicycle. It would have been too risky.

Finally, Ilmar saw some people coming out of the town hall. He counted six in all, but he couldn't tell who they were because the fog was so thick and they were so far away. Then, he heard a truck in Linnamäe going toward Keedika, a small hamlet in their township. What should he do now? Should he come out of the field to get his bicycle? Was the town hall now empty of the NKVD officers? Could he move closer and find out what was going on?

As he crept nearer, he saw Meeta, his wife Miralda's sister, standing in front of the town hall. Ilmar whistled to her. She was crying, but she recognized his whistle and saw his bicycle, so she knew it was him. "Is the coast clear?" he asked her quietly.

But she was agitated and sobbing uncontrollably. She blurted out that her husband, Kutt, had been arrested. "You are on the list to be taken too," she said. She wasn't sure if Arnold's name was on the list.

After hearing this, Ilmar rushed home to Räägu, to warn Arnold and the upstairs tenants, the Krupp family. Hearing her husband's news, Miralda put their three-month-old daughter Helle into the baby carriage and hurriedly left on foot for her parents' house in Vedra Küla, after only a hasty goodbye.

Ilmar went back to meet his friends in Linnamäe. Ago and Herbert were there with three or four other men. They tried to plan how to attack the NKVD truck carrying Kutt and the others who had been arrested. The problem was that the truck had seven men with high-powered automatic weapons, while Ilmar and his friends only had three guns and some pistols.

This is how on July 4, 1941, the NKVD forces started arresting people in the township. Twelve individuals were on their list, but the NKVD only captured five. Kutt, the first to be arrested, was deported to Siberia and shot to death in May 1942. Two other men were also arrested from the township that day and would die in the horrendous conditions of the slave labor camps. The next man to be arrested was a farmer from the hamlet of Jalukse, about ten kilometers away. After that, the truck went past them again toward Räägu Manor.

The NKVD had found and forced the town supervisor to show them where all the men on the list lived. But by the time they reached Ilmar's home, Miralda and everyone else had gone and Ilmar was hiding in the bushes.

The NKVD truck stopped some distance away from Räägu. Four men got out and went toward the house. There was only one person at home, Mrs. Krupp, the tenant who lived upstairs. She came out to meet them.

The men asked her, "Where is Ilmar?"

"He went to Tallinn three days ago," she said, "to buy machine parts to repair the mill. He hasn't come back yet."

The men forced her to sign a paper attesting to the truth of her statements. Then they told her, "When Ilmar returns, tell him he must go to the local police station, or Haapsalu, to the Russian War Commissariat."

July 4, 1941 was the beginning date for what Ilmar later termed his "borrowed life." He often wondered why he was given this loan, this reprieve. Was it fate or, perhaps, blind luck? Ilmar felt he had no inherent right to anything more than those who were arrested. He was not nobler than they were, nor more righteous. For them, it was bad luck; for Ilmar, it just happened to be better luck for him that day.

Ilmar had been officially branded as an "outlaw" and a "bandit" by the Russian occupation forces. Still, he and his comrades always referred to themselves as *metsavennad*, the Forest Brothers, or *lindpiid* ("outlaws").

Instead of allowing himself to be arrested and executed, he fled to the forest.

What became of the men they had watched roll by that night in the back of the open NKVD truck?

Juhan Silde	Died in a prison camp, February 19, 1942. In Molotov region.
Elmar Maran	Died April 17, 1942. In Kirovi region. He had been sentenced to be shot on July 27, 1942, but didn't live long enough to be executed.
Villem Leispere	Shot on April 24, 1942. In Sverdlovski region.
Johannes Kamarik	Died in a prison camp, August 4, 1942. In Norillagis.
Johannes Hein	Died in a prison camp, August 21, 1942.

Aleksander Pais	Shot on May 21, 1942.
August (Kutt) Allmäe	Shot on May 22, 1942. In Irkutski region.
Johannes Ment	Died in a prison camp, August 22, 1943. In Irkutski region

Lumiste, A. 1996. *Orult Siberisse.* Oru Vallavalitsus.

Chapter 20

Forest Brothers, Together Again, "Outlaws" All

Even with the news blackout the Soviets had imposed, the Forest Brothers finally heard of Hitler's betrayal of the Nazi–Soviet Pact with his ally Stalin with the famous Operation Barbarossa attack and that the Nazis and the Soviets were now at war. Germans had invaded the Baltics earlier in July, and the Forest Brothers forces also fought to drive the Soviets out.

The Forest Brothers believed that the Allied Forces would win and that the 1939 prewar borders would be restored. This was their hope, and it kept them going. But what if the Nazis occupied Estonia too? The Estonians in the woods had no idea what that would mean for them and their loved ones.

The death squads (*hävitamispataljonid*), paramilitary units under the control of the Soviet NKVD, continued to carry out deadly operations. They looted Estonians' homes and killed those they found. These tactics were part of a scorched-earth campaign ordered by Stalin and carried out by the retreating Russians.

July 24, 1941

Something was falling onto Ilmar's closed eyes. He wiped his face and sat up. Two birds above him were fighting or mating, shaking off bits of an overhanging branch. Ilmar felt dampness along his left side. He had rolled out from under the tattered tarp in his sleep, and the morning dew was wet against his clothing. The three others he'd slept alongside still slept—snoring, undisturbed by the birds.

The sun rose slowly. Shafts of light streamed through the treetops. A new day dawned—what would it bring? Ilmar took a knife and a piece of wood from a small bag lying next to his head. He carved another notch in the tree under which he had slept for his twentieth day as a *lindprii*: an outlaw. Ilmar never expected to go into hiding at all; he'd had nothing to fear or to hide. He was an innocent private citizen.

He found some food left by local people in small bags. Farmers on their way to their hayfields often hid food supplies in agreed-upon places. This trove consisted of a crust of bread and some smoked mutton. It was hard to find food because the Forest Brothers had to be constantly moving to evade the death squads that hunted them.

Getting food was an organized endeavor. Everyone had specific tasks. The menu usually included dried and smoked fish, ham, or mutton, and bread. Friends and relatives sometimes risked their lives by delivering food to the men in the woods. There were also contacts with nearby farmers who cooked and baked things and purposely left their pantry windows unlocked, allowing the Forest Brothers to find food. Ilmar felt degraded that he was stealing food—as if he were a common criminal lurking in the night for what he could find.

In the beginning, there were only two or three of them hiding in the woods. But after the mass deportations and the forcible draft into the Red Army, the ranks of *lindpriid* with Ilmar swelled to more than sixty and then to over one hundred. There were groups like this all over the country.

The summer had been hot and dry, and this day also promised to be warm. Some men had built small huts and shanties topped with turf dug from the heath. All the men washed in deep water holes and pits they had dug into the peat bogs. They were afraid to go near the lake where they might be spotted.

That same day, July 24, Miralda was helping with the farm work at her sister Ida's farm. Tall oaks lined the edge of the field. The oak trees gave the farm its name: Tamme Talu ("the Oaks Farm"). Even early in the morning, the sun was high in the July sky. The hay was tall, and dew glistened in the sunlight. Miralda's scythe cut through the hay. The air was clear. Her thoughts went anxiously to Ilmar, hiding in the woods, always on the move, sleeping fully dressed on the hard ground with no pillow or mattress.

Soviet death squads, knowing the German troops were marching toward them, continued to vengefully sweep out into the bogs and swamps hunting for bands of Estonian men who continued to defend their country. Packs of "bandits," the Russians called them. But the Russian occupiers were the real bandits, stealing everything they had. The Russians turned white into black and black into white, lying about everything. Miralda could not understand how anyone could believe their lies.

After constantly leaning forward from cutting hay, she stood up to stretch her back. This task was hard on her body, which had just given birth three months before. But she was glad to be able to help her sister, whose husband Kusta was with the same Forest Brothers partisan group as Ilmar.

As Miralda stretched, she saw two men approaching from the direction of the house. Her stomach churned; her limbs froze. The men were clearly coming for her, but she could not run or hide. As they neared, she could see they were carrying rifles. Miralda didn't recognize them. They wore tall boots with gray jackets that were open in the front and hung down over their trousers. Clearly, they were Russians. Who knew what they would do now that their influence over the country was coming to an end? They would not take defeat peacefully.

The soldiers lifted their guns and pointed them at Miralda. Her heart pounded, and she choked as the churning in her stomach gagged her. It crossed her mind that she might never see her beloved Ilmar again. Over the last three weeks, she'd seen him only a few times and then only briefly late at night.

She had to see him again. She had to see her baby daughter Helle. Despite her frozen limbs, despite the guns, Miralda pulled back from her work to flee. But they shouted: "*Stoi! Stoi!*" ("Stop, stop!") They asked her who she was. She heard her name spoken out to them. It didn't feel like her voice was coming from her.

The thin taller one told her in heavily Russian-accented Estonian to put down the scythe and any knives she may have under her apron. The scythe fell limply from her hand. The blood pumped through her temples as it rushed through her head. Would they shoot her? Would they rape her? What would happen next?

The short stocky one with round jowls just stared at her. He reeked of garlic. The tall one pointed her toward the road. She told him that her baby was at her parents' home with her niece and that she needed to see if the baby was all right. They consented.

She led them through the woods toward her parents' house, avoiding the road. It would have been humiliating to be seen being led like this at gunpoint like some common criminal. The three made their way through the brush and the woods. Terrible thoughts swarmed in Miralda's head. What now? Would they take only her? Would they take her parents? Her baby, little Helle?

She saw Meeta, Ida's daughter, with Helle in her arms as they approached the house. Tears rose in Miralda's throat as she saw her little daughter, the girl's golden blond hair shining in the sun. She wondered if this would be the last time she saw Helle, her parents, her brothers, or her sisters. Again, she wondered if she would ever see Ilmar again. Try as she might, she couldn't stop sobbing.

Meeta saw them coming. She ran into the house with the baby. The men told Miralda to go inside too. She and the men walked through the front door into the living room. Meeta was in the back bedroom hiding with Helle, who was crying. Maybe she had sensed Meeta's terror. Miralda told the men that she must go to her baby and that she was still breastfeeding. The men said no.

"There's no time for that now," the tall one said.

Then he asked if there was any food. Miralda told him there was nothing prepared, but she could bring them some bread and milk. They nodded yes.

As she started toward the pantry, the tall one jumped and grabbed her arm. She froze. What was he going to do to her? He pointed with his head for her to go back. "I'll get it myself," he said.

Miralda walked back to the table. The other Russian stood still, watching her. He kept looking at her all over. Her whole body shuddered, and a chill went through her. The tall one returned with a loaf of bread and a milk pail. He asked for cups and plates. Miralda pointed to the cupboard in the corner. They tore the bread apart with their hands and stuffed it into their mouths.

They ordered Miralda to sit down. Meeta was still unable to quiet Helle. Miralda pleaded with them to let her go to her baby. They shook their heads no.

The tall one asked her, "When did you last see your husband?"

"Not for three or four weeks," she answered.

"You're lying! You're lying!" he shouted. "Where is he? You do know where he is."

The other one leaned forward, stared into her face, and said, "If you don't tell us, we'll take the baby by her feet and bash her head against the wall. It's up to you."

Again, Miralda sobbed. She hated for these men to see her cry, but she couldn't stop. "Don't hurt her, please, please! She's only three months old." She began to bargain desperately and to lie to them. "Look, I'll help you get my husband." Then she spun out a lie she hoped they would believe. "I don't love him anyway. We had to get married. I was pregnant. I'll get him for you, but please don't hurt Helle! I don't know where he is now. He's somewhere in the great bog. I don't know where. But I will find out. Just give me some time."

The men conferred in Russian. Finally, the tall one said, "Okay, here's the deal. Three days from today, at exactly noon, a car will come from Haapsalu toward Linnamäe. Wait for it in front of Räägu Manor. Give the driver an envelope containing a note with the exact location of your husband and his pack of bandits, and then neither you nor your baby will be harmed."

"I can do that," Miralda promised immediately.

They finished all the bread and drank the whole pail of milk.

"Remember, Thursday, noon, exactly," the tall one said. He pushed a piece of paper in front of her that looked like a contract or a summons. It was in Russian. She could not read any of it, but she signed it anyway, her fingers trembling, her body shaking.

After they left, Miralda pushed the door to the back bedroom open. Meeta sat hunched over on the bed, her red dress stained with tears, both hers and Helle's. She looked up at Miralda. Her whole body shook. "What happened?" Meeta asked.

Miralda told her that she'd fed the men bread, milk, and a big lie. "I only feel bad about the bread and the milk," Miralda told Meeta. "These Russians live on lies. Let them savor this one. Now I must join the men in the woods myself or I am dead."

Meeta handed Helle up to Miralda's waiting arms. Miralda opened her blouse and offered the baby her breast. Baby Helle calmed down at last.

Still trembling, Miralda held her baby close. How good it was just to be alive and to be together again clutching little Helle.

On the same day Miralda was approached—July 24, 1941—the NKVD took three other women from Linnamäe into custody. Ada, Lemmi, and Alma were all wives of men in Ilmar's band of resistance fighters. As Alma's train moved through Estonia toward Russia, a bomb hit it. The train derailed, and Alma escaped. She ran into the woods and managed to get to a farmhouse. From there, she was directed to a local camp of resistance fighters.

Lemmi's father and stepmother were also arrested on the same day, along with Ilmar's brother Arnold and his wife Hilda. All four were released five days later. In the middle of the night, they were told to go home, perhaps because the Germans were approaching.

Of the three original women taken, Ada and Lemmi were deported to Siberia. They survived their ordeal in the slave labor camp and were released in 1947. They were, however, once again sent back to the camps as part of the mass deportations in Estonia that later occurred on March 23 and 24, 1949. These deportations involved over sixty thousand people from all over Estonia, who were brutally dragged from their homes during waves of nighttime terror.

Lemmi was a stunningly beautiful young woman with golden blond hair and clear blue eyes. In 1937, the noted Estonian artist Ants Laikmaa painted a portrait of her that still hangs in the Estonian Art Museum (Eesti Kunstimuuseum, KUMU) with the title "Linnamäe Lemmi." When released in 1947, she had a four-year-old daughter and was again pregnant. After her second arrest in 1949, she was taken with her youngest, then one and a half-year old. Her older daughter happened to be at her grandparents' when Lemmi was taken. Later, these grandparents were able to retrieve the younger child from Siberia.

Lemmi finally returned to Estonia in 1969, eighteen years after her first arrest that day in 1941, along with more children, who were the product of rape and sexual assault by the Russian slave labor camp guards. She returned to home as a broken and ailing woman. She and her children, marked by the stigma of having been fathered by Russian prison guards, were scorned and shunned by the local townspeople.

Not-always-accurate news of arrests reached the Forest Brothers. Ilmar was told that his brother Arnold, Arnold's wife Hilda, Lemmi, and also Miralda were among those arrested.

In despair, Ilmar determined to go to town and shoot himself in the head while standing in front of the town hall. Then, perhaps, the Russians would finally stop torturing his wife, family, and friends. The other Forest Brothers calmed him down. They convinced him to stay and see how things unfolded, arguing that they had no clear evidence of what was happening. Everything was rumors and hearsay. Later, Ilmar learned his brothers in the woods assigned someone to watch him constantly so he could not sneak away.

More information was needed. Ilmar wasn't sure whether the stories about Miralda and tiny Helle were true. So that night, after dark, accompanied by two other men, he returned home.

The doors had been sealed with wax to detect if anyone tried to enter. Ilmar didn't want to break these seals, so he peered in through the windows. He saw that their apartment at the east end of Räägu Manor had been completely ransacked. All the drawers had been emptied onto the floor as if someone were looking for something. The furniture lay strewn about the room. The place was a total mess.

Ilmar and his friends then went to his in-laws' house, not far away. He crouched down in the bushes outside of the house. The place seemed to be empty. Thoughts raced through his mind: Had they all been taken? Deported? Shot? Then he saw through the window that someone was lighting *pabeross* (a Russian cigarette, a homemade cigarette with a wad of tobacco rolled up into newspaper). Ilmar couldn't tell who it was. He feared that it might be NKVD.

But he had to find out what had happened to his family. He had to take a chance. He threw a piece of dirt up at the window. The first piece missed. He tried again. This time the clump of dirt hit the center of the windowpane. The person came toward the window, moving slowly and hesitantly. But who was there? Ilmar told his friends to be ready with rifles to protect him if it was NKVD. He squinted hard through the darkness. The figure stood at the window. Now what? Should he run? Say something? Then he heard a voice call, "Ilmar!"

To Ilmar's sheer joy, delight, and relief, it was his father-in-law, Jaan. "*Kas on puhas*?" Ilmar asked. ("Is it clear?")

"*Õhk on puhas*," he answered. ("All is clear.")

Ilmar crawled closer to the window and asked where his wife and Helle were and what had become of the others.

Jaan said Helle was with her aunt Meeta at a neighbor's house. He told Ilmar about the Russians accosting Miralda but that they hadn't taken her into custody. But then, Jaan told how Miralda had kept her freedom by lying to the Russians and tricking them. Jaan said she was now hiding from them with her sister Meeta and brother Bernhard in a barn farther away from the house. When he and Miralda's mother Anna had come home from their hayfields and had learned about what had happened, they quickly helped her get away. They also tried to get word to Ilmar so that he could come after her and take her with him to the woods.

Ilmar stood looking straight up at the moon and stars, the vastness of the sky, as relief flowed through him. Wiping away tears from his face, he reflected on what a hard, horrific day his twentieth as a *lindprii* had been, but now he felt only sweet relief.

His mother-in-law Anna came out of the house and hugged him. She quickly gathered a few things for Miralda and then took Ilmar to the barn where his wife was hiding.

Trembling, they clutched one another. They were happy just to be alive and to be together again. Miralda then had no choice but to join the Forest Brothers in the woods. *Lindpriid* all, outlaws all.

This is the Ants Laikmaa painting of "Linnamae Lemmi."

This is a photo of my mother, Miralda, taken at about the same time as the Laikmaa painting was done.

Chapter 21

The Partisan Fight from the Woods

August 1941

The fate of the other women arrested that day, the years of suffering and horror, would have been Miralda's fate, if she had not lied to buy some time and save herself. Now she found herself as the only woman with the men in the woods. She put her hair under a boy's hat and dressed like a man. Most of the others were not even aware of who she really was.

Ilmar and Miralda kept worrying about three-and-a-half-month-old Helle. Miralda wanted to return to see her baby, but Ilmar felt it would be too dangerous. Finally, Ilmar relented after seeing how much pain Miralda was feeling. He promised to see what he could find out about how Helle was doing. He left Miralda with Kustas, her brother-in-law, and went alone to his in-laws' home.

The house was bordered on two sides by pasture. There was a row of trees and bushes on the back side behind the house. He made his way along the trees, crawling on his stomach most of the way. He decided to go during daylight. He feared that at night the

NKVD would be watching for him, especially around his in-laws' place or at his home, Räägu Manor. In fact, Russian guards were posted in the park that surrounded the manor.

As he snuck toward his in-laws' house, he heard a child crying in the distance. He crept closer and closer through bushes. As he finally got close enough to the house, he saw Miralda's mother Anna walking back and forth in the yard. She clutched Helle in her arms. Both were crying. When she got closer to Ilmar, he whistled and raised his hands into the air. When she saw him, she began crying even harder.

"Oh, thank God! Thank God that at least one of you can see Helle alive perhaps for the last time." Anna handed Helle to Ilmar. He held her close. The wind blew her blond hair against his face, and the hair tickled his nose. Helle's face had a green hue. She was very sick, due, no doubt, to her having so abruptly been taken off her mother's milk and given cow's milk instead.

Anna told Ilmar that the death squad had ransacked their house soon after Miralda was supposed to meet the NKVD patrol and give them the envelope containing directions to their hiding place in the woods. They did so to Miralda's brother Volli's home as well.

Furthermore, the family faced harassment and physical threats. The NKVD officers and Russian soldiers had forced Miralda's father, Jaan, to run across a field while they fired their rifles at his feet. Suddenly, he turned toward them. Standing tall and squaring his shoulders, he declared, "During the War of Independence, I was an Estonian freedom fighter. Go ahead and shoot if that satisfies you. I'm not running anymore." The soldiers conferred among themselves, lowered their guns, and let him go.

Ema's mother, Anna, was also assaulted. They put her against the house wall and held a rifle to her head. They demanded that she tell them where her son hid in the woods. One of the NKVD men held a knife to her throat and said, "If you don't tell us where they are, we will cut out your tongue!" She answered, "If you do that, I won't be able to say anything or tell you where anyone is hiding."

Walking back to the camp, Ilmar was sickened by all this news. What should he do? Should he tell the truth to Miralda about how sick little Helle was and the torture their loved ones were suffering, or should he lie? Miralda would want to see Helle and her family if he told the truth. Maybe she would want to bring Helle back into the woods with them. But that would be impossible, and possibly it was too late for that now, anyway.

When he returned to the camp, he saw Miralda standing by the scrub pines. He went over to her and gave her as much of a reassuring hug as he could muster. "Everything's okay," he whispered. "They are all okay. Little Helle is fine."

How could he lie like this? He felt horrible for the next three days. Maybe he should have told the truth. Surely, she would learn the truth and know that he'd lied. And then, would she ever trust him again? Why should she?

He couldn't stand it any longer, so he sent Kustas back to learn how things were going. Kustas returned with good news. Helle was feeling better now. Her grandmother had given Helle some drinking shots of *puskar* (moonshine alcohol). Perhaps this had helped her to recover; maybe the recovery was the alcohol or fate or a powerful merciful force that spared their baby.

With only one woman in the camp, both Miralda and the other men were somewhat uncomfortable. So, she and Ilmar kept their little distance from the others. They slept together on the peat bog surrounded in the three- to four-foot-high grasses with colorful heather on top on narrow rubber strips they laid on the ground beneath them.

One morning, Ilmar opened his eyes to see a long, giant, black snake slowly slithering between them, going straight for Miralda's face. He held his breath, afraid to move, afraid he'd scare the snake into striking. After a long time, it finally left, slinking off into the grass.

The morning was chilly and cloudy, but even so Ilmar was sweating. The thought of the snake biting and possibly poisoning Miralda gripped him. Because of the snakes, the tall grass was not safe for them to sleep. He woke his wife and said, "We need to find a safer, better place to stay."

Not far from the campsite, they found a barn half-filled with hay. While it was safer from snakes, they were now more out on their own. Camp guards were assigned to shifts all day and night to look for danger surrounding them.

The door to the barn had been tightly nailed shut. Ilmar and Miralda left it as it was. At the back of the building, they lifted some loose stones from the foundation. Once inside, they rolled the rocks back into the hole so no one could tell it had been disturbed.

Ilmar was worried because right next to the barn was a well-worn path that had been recently used. *Perhaps the death squads were using it*, he thought.

He and Miralda used the barn only at night to sleep. The thick stands of trees, the brush, and tall grass were where they spent their days. The death squad raids came during the daytime, so hiding in the trees was much safer than being in the barn. At night, however, the barn provided them with good cover. Sleeping in the barn was better than on the ground. The hay was soft. They were sheltered from the mid August nights, which were growing chillier.

As the fall days grew shorter, the nights became longer and colder. Ilmar agonized over what was going to happen to them. How long would they have to stay in the woods? With the weather getting colder, the temperature would drop. How would they manage? How would they survive? Would they ever be able to come out of the woods and go home again? Would life ever return to normal? Would this horror ever end?

As Ilmar and Miralda hid in the bushes, they helped Kustas weave baskets by peeling pine roots for him to use as he wove. They were all quiet, absorbed in their thoughts.

They had one frying pan and a big black pot. They had rolled stones together as a makeshift stove. Ilmar wanted to start a fire to cook some blueberries soup they could eat with pancakes left over from breakfast. But Kustas wanted to finish making his basket.

Then they heard some noise from the path next to the barn. Suddenly, they heard automatic gunfire. The Forest Brothers didn't have such weapons, so the three knew these weren't their men firing. It had to be a raid by the Russian NKVD.

The three grabbed their guns and strained to see what was happening. The sound of the shots came from the main campsite. Because of the hot weather, Ilmar had taken off his high boots. So now he stood there, barefoot, single-shot rifle in hand, ready to take on the NKVD death squad.

The three hid in a clump of brush and small, scraggly pine trees. Ilmar told Kustas and Miralda to stay there, not to move, and that he would see what was happening. He returned to the barn to put his boots back on.

One of the Estonian men, Eduard Pere, was sleeping in the barn. It was good that he didn't snore because the Russians had just passed by no more than fifteen feet away. Now he was awake. "What's going on? What's going on?" he whispered.

Shots started to hit the side of the barn and the roof. Ilmar didn't see anyone when he peered through a crack, so he returned to where he'd left Kustas and Miralda. They were gone. Now shots came from all different directions. Ilmar sank down onto his knees. He tried to whistle, but nothing happened. His mouth was too dry, and calling out was too dangerous.

He saw smoke rising. It filled the sky like a dark cloud. The Russians had set the shanties and huts at the main campsite on fire. Ilmar climbed up a small pine tree. The air was filled with gunfire. Bullets whistled by him on all sides. Out on the bog, he saw NKVD men moving toward the smoking campsite. The death squad members slowly walked past him in a column of perhaps one hundred men. They would have found Ilmar, Miralda, and Kustas if he had lit the campfire to make soup earlier. Was it fate, happenstance, or grace that he had not made the fire during this onslaught?

Ilmar clung to the pine tree which swung from side to side under his weight. He strained to spot Kustas and Miralda. Where could they be? Fearing he could be seen, he dropped to the ground and made his way back to the tall shrubs and grass. His heart leapt when he finally found his wife and her father lying on their stomachs hidden in the tall grass. They described how, during the onslaught, they hoped to make an escape by rushing across an open area into a taller stand of trees.

Miralda had been wearing a bright-colored sweater pulled over her clothes, which was visible from a distance. She had removed the sweater and carefully rolled it into a tight ball. As she did this, a large contingent of Russians crossed the opening.

The three of them dropped to their stomachs in the tall grass and lay motionless as these large groups of death squad soldiers marched past them. Some holes had been dug into the bog as hiding places. They crawled into these holes and pulled moss, brush, and grass over the top, covering them. They remained underground until nightfall, when all became safe and quiet.

The Germans took Tallinn from the Soviets on August 21, 1941, but the retreating Russians continued to commit crimes in the rural areas. Eventually, Germany occupied Estonia and incorporated it into its Reichskommisariat Osland (the civilian occupation regime in Lithuania, Latvia, and Estonia). At first, Estonians were relieved to have been freed from Soviet terror. But it soon became apparent that they had again fallen under the control of a deadly, devastating, and destructive occupation.

During the ongoing chaos, the Forest Brothers continued to fight to safeguard and defend Estonian citizens from the retreating NKVD death squads. As part of this effort, on the early morning of August 31, 1941, Ilmar and his friend Ago rode a motorcycle with an attached side cart into the coastal city of Haapsalu. They were ragged with long scraggly beards from having just spent weeks in the woods. They rode down the middle of Posti Tänav (the main street). Ago steered while Isa held a machine gun up to his shoulder, slowly sweeping it from side to side as they rode.

Everything was calm and peaceful in the city. And so, they decided to go to Palivere, a beautiful nearby manor that the Russians had used as a command post. They wanted to make sure the Russians were leaving ahead of the German occupation. Riding along narrow, secluded forest roads to avoid being detected, they met friends near the village of Keedika and left their motorcycle there to exchange it for a car.

As they approached Palivere Manor, they saw NKVD activity around the manor park. Soviets were moving out quickly, packing things into trucks as they withdrew before the German occupation. A sentry heard them coming. The Russians opened fire.

Ilmar ran from the car through a hail of machine-gun bullets and crouched behind a stone wall. Bullets whistled all around him. It felt surreal, but the deadly shots zooming past his head were as real as it gets. It was as though he had stuck his head into a beehive. Through his mind flashed thoughts that this would be his end.

In addition to the machine-gun fire, there were outbursts of mortar shells that struck and exploded all around them. One shot hit an evergreen tree right in front of him. It bore a five-inch hole through the middle of the tree. The tree stood straight up like a Christmas tree secured in a stand for a moment before crashing.

Badly outnumbered, Ilmar and Ago fired back and were quickly becoming surrounded. They dashed back to their car, jumped in, and sped away, ducking low onto the seats.

Again, they followed narrow wooded lanes. They made it safely to Vedra Küla ("Vedra village") and Aru Talu, Ema's childhood home. Pulling into the yard, Ilmar saw Miralda standing in the doorway. He leaped out of the car before it even stopped, ran over, and held her tightly. He said, "At Palivere, none of the Russian bullets were meant for me today." He whispered to her that they would soon return home and live with their daughter Helle again.

Ema süda	**A Mother's Heart**
Üks paigake siin ilmas on, Kus varjul truudus, arm ja õnn. Kõik, mis nii harv siin ilma peal, On pelgupaiga leidnud seal. Kõik, mis nii harv siin ilma peal, On pelgupaiga leidnud seal.	There's a place in this world Where there's faithfulness, grace, and happiness. All that's so rare in this world has found a safe haven there. All that's so rare in this world has found a safe haven there.
Kas ema südant tunned sa? Nii õrn, nii kindel, muutmata. Ta sinu rõõmust rõõmu näeb, Su õnnetusest osa saab Ta sinu rõõmust rõõmu näeb, Su õnnetusest osa saab	Do you know a mother's heart? So tender, so sure, unchanged. It takes joy in your happiness and takes part in your accidents. It takes joy in your happiness and takes part in your accidents.
Mõnd kallist südant kaot´sin, Mis järel´ nuttes leinasin. Aeg andis teist mul tagasi, Ei emasüdant iialgi Aeg andis teist mul tagasi, Ei emasüdant iialgi	Many dear hearts I did lose, which I missed and mourned. Time gave back the second one, but a mother's heart never. Time gave back the second one, but a mother's heart never.

Chapter 22

Aho's Story: A Long Trek Along the Tracks

Once the Soviets were gone, the Germans disarmed the Forest Brothers, and my parents were able to apply to return to their home. My father and uncle successfully petitioned to have their property returned, including Räägu Manor, forty hectares of farmland and gardens, and a gristmill. My sister Tiia was born during this time in 1942.

My father and uncle were never drafted into the German army because the Germans needed fresh food and flour to feed their troops. In this way, they were more valuable to the Germans. They sold produce and flour that the Germans badly needed for a low price. During the German occupation, they maintained a low profile and were careful not to violate any rules or upset their new occupiers.

But by 1944, the Germans were losing the war.

As the Nazis scrambled to survive in the final months of World War II, they left their occupied territories undefended. Before

Germany finally surrendered in May 1945, the Soviets moved to reoccupy Estonia and the Baltics in September 1944.

The threat of another Soviet occupation terrified everyone. Many had heard the horrific stories of the Russian gulags and became desperate to leave.

Here is one such story. The story is true, but identifying information has been changed to protect anonymity and privacy.

As the Soviets again conquered Estonia in 1944, Aho [not his real name] was pulled out of his home in the middle of the night by armed Russian members of a death squad. His brothers and sisters had already managed to escape to Sweden.

Deported by train in a boxcar, Aho was taken to one of the Soviet gulag camps in the Perm region, a heavily forested area of the Ural Mountains close to Siberia.

Aho's camp was in Udmurtia, where the aboriginal people of this region, the Udmurts, live, and whose language is Finno-Ugrian, similar to other Permian languages and Aho's native Estonian.

These were logging camps. Aho's camp was like thousands of other slave labor camps throughout the Soviet Union.

A typical day consisted of wake-up sirens at six in the morning with a scant breakfast at six-thirty. The roll call was at seven. At seven thirty, they marched for an hour and a half, deep into the forests with armed Russian guard escorts. The workday consisted of cutting trees by hand using axes and frame saws and cutting the lumber into manageable pieces that could be floated down the Kama River to the Volga in the spring after the ice melted.

After hours of harsh, grueling, physical labor, at six in the evening, the prisoners were marched the hour and a half back to camp. At seven thirty, they were provided a meal, often consisting of watery, brothy soup with a few vegetables floating in it and sometimes small pieces of fish or meat.

At eight, they did various hard labor around the camp, such as chopping firewood or shoveling snow. At eleven, the lights went off. This routine was the same through the days, weeks, months, and years for the inmates.

Aho's camp consisted of four barracks and housed about 250 prisoners. There was also a punishment block (for prisoners who disobeyed the harsh camp rules), a first aid station, outhouses, and a headquarters building.

Inmates regularly died from beatings, overwork, and lack of nutrition. A constant flow of newly arriving prisoners continually filled the ranks of those who had died.

Russian guards checked the barracks for the dead late at night and early in the morning. These corpses were then dragged to the wall surrounding the camp and tossed over the barbed wire into big piles outside. The bodies lay there frozen until the spring thaw, slowly deteriorating, often torn apart and eaten by animals. In the spring, prisoners were sent out in groups to bury these remains in large nearby pits.

After months of this, Aho was so weak that he passed out late one night. The guards thought he was dead. They pulled him out of his cot, dragged him to the wall, and threw him onto the bodies below. The sudden cold shocked him awake. He scavenged for clothing from the bodies, and, although the urge revolted him, he even stooped to chewing chunks of flesh to ease his hunger.

So as not to be detected by the guards stationed in the corner tower, Aho crawled on his stomach across the clearing to the dense shrubs and into the shadow of the woods.

After wandering through the woods, he found the railway tracks that had brought him there from Estonia. He surmised that if he walked along these tracks heading west, he could return home, about 1,400 miles away.

He couldn't risk walking during the daylight. Locals were offered monetary rewards for sighting escaped prisoners and notifying authorities. He slept under dense brush during the day and walked through the long winter nights. Aho stole clothes hanging on clotheslines to get something dry to wear. He only took one or two items at a time so that perhaps the owners wouldn't notice. When he came upon an empty house, he broke in carefully without making it noticeable and stole food and drink, stuffing as much as he could into his pockets.

During the shorter nights of summer, his time for walking decreased. It took Aho almost two years to return home. But finally, he walked across the border from Russia into Estonia. The train tracks had led him back home.

His joy was cut short by the crude reality and realization that he couldn't be seen openly in public. He remained in hiding for several years until Stalin's death, when amnesty for many prisoners was proclaimed.

He lived in hiding under an assumed name, helped by people to get food, clothing, and odd jobs. Most people feared and did not trust him because he had mysteriously returned from the gulag. People feared he might have been compromised, and he was now a *koputaja*, a KGB informant.

Aho was now back in his beloved homeland. But his loved ones were gone. His five brothers and sisters had escaped to the West. He no longer had a home. He was alone, isolated from others, living under an assumed name, and still disgusted by what he was forced to do to stay alive while on that pile of corpses. He was a hollow shell, a measure of the toll taken by the horrors of the gulag and his long trek along the tracks.

Chapter 23

Uncle Arnold: Survival and Loss

So, with the specter of Soviet reoccupation looming, my parents and sisters fled on September 22, 1944, at the last minute, in that small wooden boat bound for Sweden across the Baltic Sea. The Soviets would be fully in charge by September 26. After being caught in the storm for four days, my family was rescued at the last minute from their sinking boat by the Swedish navy.

My parents' experiences reflect the intense, painful, and harrowing times during these occupations, with their need to hide for weeks in the woods, their resourcefulness in dealing with the Germans, and the agonizing decision to flee before the second Russian occupation. The decision to escape was painful and heart-wrenching and not what they wanted. It meant leaving everything and everybody behind.

Sadly, they never saw many members of their family again. They did not want to leave Estonia, but they could not remain. The Russians had branded them as enemies of the people in 1941 because they had escaped being arrested. Had they stayed in Estonia, they would have undoubtedly faced either lengthy prison time or execution.

September 1944

As my mother described before, my uncle Arnold and his family were also on that boat. But as Isa and his brother struggled to get the engine running, Hilda, Arnold's wife, made her fateful decision.

The *Ahti* was packed with people. The insides were covered with the deep red clay from when it rested at the harbor's bottom. As Arnold and Ilmar struggled to get the motor running, Arnold felt a tug at his coat.

He turned to see Hilda standing behind him. She said, "We can't go to Sweden in this boat. We'll die. I dreamt that you were out in the fields plowing when the walls fell on the children and me all at once. Look at this boat. We'll never make it across the Baltic! I'm staying here, and so are the kids." She leaned forward into the engine room. She looked first at Arnold and then at Ilmar. "I'm not going out onto the sea to die. What are you going to do?"

Ilmar replied, "It makes no difference whether I die at sea or we go back and are killed by the Russians on land. At least by going, we have a chance."

Hilda grabbed the bags and pulled the children—their daughters, Milvi and Leili, and their son, Toivo—out of the boat. Arnold had no choice but to help her with the bags and start walking back toward the town.

Walking along the beach, about an hour later, they met a man who turned out to be Danish. He had worked at Taebla Manor.

Hilda spoke enough German to communicate with him. He told Hilda that a small rowboat was coming from Vormsi Island and was taking another family to Vormsi. From there, they hoped to get to Saaremaa Island, where ships could still launch.

Soon the boat arrived, and everyone squeezed into it. The adults took turns rowing the ten kilometers out to Vormsi Island.

The following morning, the Soviets were already in Rohuküla and, with artillery, were shelling Vormsi Harbor. A strong storm developed, lasting for three days. Soon, broken pieces of boats and bodies began to wash up on the beach. Arnold dreaded the thought of seeing his brother Ilmar, his wife, and their two little daughters among the debris and corpses.

The group of refugees swelled and started moving westward across the island. As they traveled, they found abandoned horses on empty farms. Some people rode these horses toward the west coast of Vormsi Island. On the way, they met an agronomist named Kaseorg from Petserimaa. He took the children onto a cart he had harnessed to a horse.

People were talking about a boat that was supposed to come from Muhumaa Island. They waited for several hours. Hope began to wane as the bombardments from the east grew louder. But finally, the boat did arrive. It was big and flat-bottomed. This allowed the boat to come close to shore. Even so, there was no place for it to dock.

So, they gathered wagons and machinery from the nearby farms and pushed them into the water, forming a makeshift pier. The winds were still gusting at times, as much as sixty meters per second. The waves crashed all around. Huddled together, they held on as tightly as possible to the ropes pulling the boat up against the jerry-rigged pier. This allowed the women and children to climb on board. Despite these attempts, the ship kept breaking loose. It took all their energy to pull it back and hold it firmly against the pier. But at last, they were all able to board.

With this boat, they made it to Muhumaa Island. They made their way on yet another boat to Saaremaa Island. They spent their first night in an abandoned store in Saaremaa. The owner had already escaped. They then went to the port of Kuressaare, about ninety kilometers away. The trip took three days. They were lucky enough to get a ride in the back of an open truck. After they arrived at the capital city Kurressaare, they looked for their old friend Mr. Kivi. They found his house, where they learned the Kivi family had fled the previous Thursday.

It was now Saturday morning. Arnold went through the market to the harbor to look for possibilities for still getting onto a ship. There, he met a family named Hip. They also wanted to escape and told them of a chance to get onto a bigger ship called the *Nordstern.* With their help, Arnold and his family could secure places on this ship. On the morning of October 3, Arnold, Hilda, and their three children boarded. On October 5, they left port alongside the *Nordstern*'s sister ship, the *Nauding.*

Because there was not enough room in the cabins below, many men spent the night trying to sleep on deck, smoking cigarettes and talking. On the morning of October 6, at about ten, Arnold was standing near the bow of the ship. Across from him stood Dr. Rumma and alongside him was Mr. Kaseorg with his ten-year-old son, Peeter.

Suddenly, a crewman yelled, "*Torpedo!*"

A massive blast shot through the middle of the ship—a torpedo shot from the Russian submarine ŠTŠ-407 captained by Botšarov.

The bow section, where the two older men and the boy stood, remained afloat for perhaps a minute and a half. Dr. Rumma yelled that his legs were shattered. Arnold shouted back that his legs were too. Later, Arnold could not remember how he had done this, but he let go of the ship's railing and grabbed a rope attached to a large round rubber life raft. Clutching the raft, he managed to hold his head above the water. He and Dr. Rumma faced each other, grasping the ropes wrapped around the raft. Little Peeter Kaseoru sat on top of the meshed strings in the middle of the raft, repeatedly reciting the Lord's Prayer.

From all around, Arnold heard people screaming for help. Some clung to small scraps of wood as they bobbed in the turbulent water. Later, Arnold was unsure how long it took before the other ship, the *Nauding*, arrived to help.

Arnold was paralyzed by pain and too weak to grasp the rope thrown down. Someone jumped overboard from the ship into the raft and wrapped the rope around his body. They pulled him up to a ladder and lifted him onto the deck. His leg was almost completely severed. Only one tendon still held it to his torso. He squirmed on the floor of the deck in sheer pain. Someone poured vodka into his mouth. A medic named Mr. Mägi broke a wooden ladder by striking it against the railing. With the wooden pieces, he made a splint on Arnold's leg. All the while, booze was poured into his mouth.

Later, Arnold learned that Dr. Rumma's leg had been amputated in Stockholm. Arnold supposed he was lucky. Although the numbers are not certain, it is possible that of the 650 people on the *Nordstern*, perhaps only about forty survived.

Sometime later, he woke up in a grimy, filthy hospital where doctors had fixed up his leg. He spent three days there. He was then moved to recover in a makeshift hospital that had been a schoolhouse. It was infested with lice and bedbugs. He didn't sleep for two weeks because of bugs crawling over him. His whole body itched relentlessly. When they finally removed his bandages and cast, they discovered that the bedbugs had eaten a hole into his leg and had built a nest.

When he finally limped and hobbled out of the hospital, he found himself in Germany, a strange, war-torn land, unable to speak the language, barely able to walk, alone, vermin infested. His wife and children, Hilda, Milvi, Leili, and Toivo, were at the bottom of the Baltic Sea.

It was December 6, 1944, Toivo's fourth birthday.

After my parents survived their dangerous journey across the Baltic, I was born in Sweden and later, as recounted, our family stopped in London, England, on the way from Sweden to Canada. At three and a half years of age, I became Arnold's godson to somehow replace his lost son Toivo.

After a year in Canada, we moved to the United States. My parents worked hard. We all toiled long hours working on our farm.

Over time, our life became more comfortable, but the deep emotional scars remained. Late at night, I often heard Isa's footsteps in the hallway near my bedroom. Sleeplessness plagued him for years. Isa never fully recovered from the guilt he felt for having survived, while death squads had killed many of the others and dear family had died at sea.

"We do not want to go, but we cannot stay." "*Minna ei taha, kuid jääda ei saa.*"

Chapter 24

My Estonian Journey Ends: A Blend of Joy and Sorrow with Sadness

During our last night in Estonia in 1974, Silja and I, along with my friend Tõnu, went to a noted meeting place for artists, writers, and intellectuals in Tallinn. A small place with stone walls, arched low ceilings, and subdued lighting, creating a cozy ambience, it was a historic underground bar and restaurant in the basement of the Tallinn Art Hall (Tallinna Kunstihoone) building.

When we arrived, Silja recognized Juhan Viiding, a prominent young Estonian poet and actor, just sitting down with his young daughter. We joined them, but the waitress refused to serve us because his daughter was at our table. At the same time, a journalist named Arnold arrived and invited all of us to his nearby apartment, where we partied late into the night.

Of course, I was familiar with Viiding's work. I couldn't believe I was in Tallinn partying with him. He was wiry, short, and thin, with long, wavy hair and somewhat disheveled. My hair and beard had grown long during several weeks in Europe, so perhaps he felt a kindred bohemian spirit with me. Walking next to Silja and me while the others strolled ahead, he made disparaging comments about the Russian occupiers filled with wit and irony, likening them to Nazis and even softly singing a few bars of an anti Soviet song. I was stunned to hear such open defiance right in front of us—we were strangers to him. I didn't know how to respond.

He drank somewhat heavily during the party, as did the journalist Arnold. Viiding was well known for his intellectual acuity and innovative and profound poetic style, which dealt with the dark themes of the human condition, identity, aloneness, and alienation. Sadly, he committed suicide in 1995 at age forty-seven, which was a tragic loss for the Estonian literary community.

The next day, my tour left by ship for Finland. For the first time, my Estonian family was there with flowers to see me off. When Uncle Volli said goodbye, he had tears in his eyes and said he missed my mother. I was deeply touched by this authentic expression of emotion coming from him. He was a big, strong, burly man with full blond hair and had worked on the railroad all his life. Ema had often described Volli as having always taken care of her and looked out for her when they were growing up.

These photos show some of my relatives seeing me off in 1974. Volli and Linda are on the right side.

After arriving in Helsinki, the next day we flew back home. My parents met me at the airport. I hugged, then grasped my father's hand firmly. Looking him straight in the eyes, I said, "*Sul oli õigus. Vene okupatsioon on veelgi hullem, kui ma ette kujutasin.*" ("You were right. The Russian occupation is even worse than I had imagined.")

My first trip to Estonia left me immensely angered, outraged, and deeply depressed by the horrific Russification that was systematically taking place. I felt I had to do something to aid my suffering, oppressed, and endangered people.

First, I certainly became more politically active. Pragmatically, I also believed that to be part of preserving my language and culture, I should eventually marry an Estonian. I worked long and hard to improve my language skills and began presenting workshops and lectures at events in Canada, New York, Washington, and elsewhere. Maybe I was just one man, but I could create a life devoted to my country. I would join with those around me to resist fearlessly.

Eestlane Olen ja Eestlaseks jään	Estonian I Am
Tuhat korda kas või alata tuhat aastat tõusu mitte luigelend oma rahvust maha salata sama ränk on nagu orjaks müüa end.	A thousand times, even without land a thousand years of ascension, not swan flight, hiding your nationality is as bad as selling yourself as a slave.
Eestlane olen ja eestlaseks jään, kui mind eestlaseks loodi. Eestlane olla on uhke ja hää vabalt vaarisa moodi.	Estonian I am and Estonian I'll remain, since I was created Estonian. Being Estonian is glorious and beautiful, free like our forefathers.
Tuhat kõuehäälset küsijat Vaba meri. Põlistalud. Püha muld. Tuhat korda tuhat püsijat kõige kiuste elus hoiab püha tuld.	A thousand loud questioners. Free sea. Native farms. Holy soil. A thousand times, a thousand stalwarts keep the sacred fire alive despite everything.
Eestlane olen ja eestlaseks jään, kui mind eestlaseks loodi. Eestlane olla on uhke ja hää vabalt vaarisa moodi.	Estonian I am and Estonian I'll remain, since I was created Estonian. Being Estonian is glorious and beautiful, free like our forefathers.
Mm . . . jah, just nõnda vabalt vaarisa moodi. Nende mehiste meeste moodi.	Mm . . . Yes, free just like our forefathers. Like those manly men.
Eestlane olen ja eestlaseks jään, kui mind eestlaseks loodi. Eestlane olla on uhke ja hää vabalt vaarisa moodi.	Estonian I am and Estonian I'll remain, since I was created Estonian. Being Estonian is glorious and beautiful, free like our forefathers.
Jah, just nõnda vabalt vaarisa moodi. Nende mehiste meeste moodi.	Yes, free just like our forefathers. Like those manly men.

Chapter 25

Finland and the 1975 Song Festival

During the trip in 1974, everyone had repeatedly urged me to return the following year, 1975, for the national song and dance festival (*Üldlaulu- ja tantsupidu*) that happened every five years.

My 1974 trip had been a meaningful, powerful, and emotional experience. But meeting relatives for the first time with the ever-present Russian occupation and oppression—the rank Russification of Estonians who have lived on this patch of land on the Baltic coast for thousands of years—filled me with distressing, empathetic pain for what they had lived through for so long. I had left feeling both exhilarated and depressed. These emotions lingered long after my return.

I started the process of getting a visa for 1975 early because it took so long to process the paperwork and get approved. I also began working on talking my good friend Tõnu into going with me. He was reluctant, but I was persistent. Finally, he agreed. We also needed to purchase festival tickets through Intourist. We planned to spend a couple of weeks in Finland before going to Estonia. My college teaching job still allowed for long summer breaks. All of this worked together to find us once again headed to Europe.

Summer 1975

Prior to going to Estonia, Tõnu and I had a good time exploring Finland together. We took the train to Turku and spent a couple of days there, but we stayed mostly in Helsinki. While in the college town of Turku, we stayed at a student dormitory where some summer school students resided.

Three Finish students invited the two of us to their room and offered us a beer. It was cordial and amicable until we discussed Estonia. Tõnu and I described the Soviet occupation of Estonia, emphasizing that the raw brutality included crimes against civilians such as raping women, murdering men, looting, and pillaging. The Soviets' policy was designed to obliterate the Estonian language and culture. The percentage of Estonians in the population had fallen from 95 percent to about 60 percent.

The Finns who had invited us to join their gathering, Matti, Juhani, and Antti, did not believe what we told them. Antti responded, "In the Soviet system, everyone is guaranteed a job, a place to live, and health care." Juhani and Antti added that the Soviets stood for peace while the United States was killing people in Vietnam.

Matti added, "Estonia has been doing well under Soviet rule. It's a worker's paradise!"

Tõnu raised an eyebrow. "A worker's paradise? Have you investigated what's been happening there?"

Juhani smirked. "But surely it can't be that bad if they call it paradise."

"Right!" Antti added. "The Soviets say they're promoting equality and workers' rights. Isn't that a good thing?"

I leaned forward. "You should read more about our history from credible sources, not state-sponsored propaganda. There's a vast difference between what's portrayed and the reality. Under Soviet occupation, we had mass deportations—families were taken from their homes and sent to labor camps just for being Estonian."

Matti frowned. "Labor camps? That sounds harsh, but maybe that's just a price for progress, right?"

"Price for progress?" Tõnu said, frustrated. "They weren't just labor camps; they were places of suffering, loss, and death. Mass arrests, executions . . . people were silenced for voicing their beliefs."

Juhani shook his head. "Come on, you must be exaggerating. I mean, every country has its tough times during transitions."

Tõnu tried to remain calm. "It's not an exaggeration. Look at the women during those times; they suffered greatly. Women were taken away, leaving families shattered, all because they wanted to preserve their culture and refused to accept Soviet ideology."

"But surely something good must come from this," Matti maintained, "if they promote workers' rights?"

I sighed. "That's ironic coming from a regime that exploits its people. It's about control, not rights. The so-called 'worker's paradise' was built on fear and oppression. It's crucial to acknowledge how many lives were destroyed by Soviet ideology. It's really just thinly veiled Russian imperialism."

Tõnu agreed. "We must share the truth about the Russian occupation of Estonian, so it isn't lost."

What had started as a friendly hangout in their dorm room, sharing a beer, turned awkward and tense. I was upset, and I struggled hard not to show it.

Tõnu and I excused ourselves, thanked our hosts for the beer, and left. I seethed with anger and spent most of the night tossing in bed, ruminating about this shocking encounter. These students were totally unaware of the rapes, murders of civilians, mass deportation. They refused to believe what we described. I was overwhelmed by the extent to which Soviet propaganda held such a grip on young Finish students and the extent of the Russian propaganda and disinformation effort.

The next day, we took the train back to Helsinki. Tõnu worked for the Canadian government and was friends with the Canadian ambassador's son. The ambassador had invited Tõnu to visit him at the Embassy. Tõnu went in for his visit while I sat in the waiting room. I noticed the secretary was an attractive blond-haired, blue-eyed woman named Anni.

The place was empty, so I began chatting with her. We had a friendly encounter. Before Tõnu came out from his visit, I arranged a double date with Anni and her friend Vivian that evening. The four of us went to a local club, where Spanish ladies danced to sensuous Latin rhythms for entertainment. Our table was in front of the stage. Suddenly, Tõnu was led to the stage by one of the dancers, where he became part of their act. Tõnu and I still laugh about his dancing in the nightclub show. We agreed to see Anni and Vivian again when we returned from Estonia the night before our flight back to Toronto.

We also frequented a primary student hangout club in central Helsinki, the "Old Cellar" in the ornate Students' Hall. It had cheap beer, concerts, live performances, and films. During the 1970s, "Finlandization" was the dominant factor. It had resulted from Finland's WWII losses to the Soviet Union and meant an accommodation and an effort not to be critical or offend the Russians. There was much censorship and self-censorship within universities and among student groups. Night after night, the club showed films depicting Americans as warmongering monsters. At the same time, the Soviets were portrayed as peace-loving people living in a society that laid out the path to a better future for the world. In such a hostile environment, I sometimes tried to pass myself off as a Canadian—after all, I'd lived in Canada. In 1974 and again in '75, I frequented this club for its cheap beer and youthful demographic.

An example of Finlandization was the private brewing company Karjala. The Soviet Union had attacked Finland in November 1939. The "Winter War," which ended in March 1940 with the Moscow Peace Treaty, forced Finland to cede Karjala to the Soviet Union. Moscow tried to get the Finnish prime minister and government to force Karjala's logo to be removed. The logo depicts two arms raised in battle, with the one on the left holding a traditional Finnish straight knife while the other arm has a traditional Russian-Mongol curved knife. This knife style dates to the Mongol rule in Russia, beginning in the 1200s and lasting two centuries. I savored Karjala beer, enhanced by delightful spite each time I ordered it.

Photo of the Karjala beer can with the two arms wielding swords.

The four-hour sail to Tallinn felt much like the one the year before. I strained to see the towers and church steeples of Tallinn. Upon arrival, we were again forced to endure the repeated inspection of our documents and scrutiny by Russian officials with whom we could not communicate. I was forced to open my suitcase inside the building, allowing the official to ransack every inch of it, pulling out a ballpoint pen and slipping it into his pocket; such pens were impossible to get in the Soviet Union. With everything pulled apart, my suitcase was hard to close again. Outside, there were relatives to greet me this time, but I wasn't allowed to speak to them because we were quickly herded into the Intourist bus. Enel, our guide, confiscated our travel documents at the bus's door. Tõnu and I went to our room past the women sitting at their desk in the lobby, noting our arrival.

This time, though, it felt more natural to be with my relatives, who seemed happy to see me and excited that I had returned to attend the national song and dance festival as they had all urged me to do. There were the usual Intourist official tours, but fewer this time. I had seen enough "thriving" collective farms and been presented with enough graphs depicting steady "growth and progress" to last me a lifetime on my last trip.

The highlight in 1975 was the national festival, which began with the flame brought from Tartu. That was the site of the first song festival in 1869, celebrating the fiftieth anniversary of the end of serfdom in Estonia in 1819. During Estonian independence from 1918 to 1940, and significantly during the Soviet occupation with its policy of Russification until 1991, song festivals played a crucial role in the country's national awakening, cultural preservation, and national identity.

With my cousin's daughter Tiiu, Tõnu and I watched the several-hours-long parade of participants through the streets of Tallinn from Freedom Square to the song festival site, about four kilometers and more than an hour's walk. I attended the dance festival on Friday, and the song festival was on Saturday and Sunday. The Lauluväljak (song festival grounds) was filled with thousands of people. The Suur Laulu Arkaad ("Great Song Arch") held over thirty thousand singers. Being in this iconic place evoked both joy and sadness—the joy of being together with so many Estonians at once and the sadness of realizing that a considerable portion of the world's total Estonian population could fit into this one space.

The Soviet censor had to approve everything in the program. And so, much of the repertoire was awful, as in "Ode for Lenin."

The massive crowd talked loudly, drank beer, ate, and slept. During the Soviet portions, people wandered around, not paying attention.

When "*Mu Isamaa on Minu Arm*" ("My Native Land, My Dearest") (Lydia Koidula's poem, set to music by Gustav Ernesaks and conducted by him that day) was announced over the sound system, everyone rose to their feet, stood silently, and bowed their heads in reverence. This song has a deep emotional connection for Estonians. It evokes a strong love and devotion to our homeland and maintained a sense of national identity and unity among Estonians, primarily through the dark days of the Soviet occupation. When it ended, the people in the audience spontaneously erupted by singing its lyrics: "*Peaksin sada surma ma . . . sa siiski elad südames.*" ("Should you, my homeland, perish, within my heart you will live on.")

The climax for me was actively participating in a mini-insurrection—standing on the bench, singing, and shouting through the blaring music the Russians played while faced with a show of force consisting of uniformed militia and dogs. For a brief time, aspirations exploded for freedom from tyranny, but as always, it was expressed through song.

We stood on the benches, shouting for Gustav Ernesaks, the composer of the iconic song "*Mu Isamaa on Minu Arm*" ("My Homeland Is My Love"), to return. The chorus of thousands began singing spontaneously even though Ernesaks was not allowed to mount the podium again to conduct. Thousands in the public joined in with joy and passion.

The singing continued even through the loud march music blared by the Russians. People spontaneously locked arms and swayed in unison, singing forbidden songs that in the past had led people to be arrested and disappear. Our safety was in the tens of thousands of people facing this small contingent of Russian troops. The situation was, however, a tinder box that threatened to ignite a physical altercation.

We all locked arms with friends, relatives, and strangers. It felt like one big family. Marika and Enel performed as singers in local clubs, which helped me stay on pitch and accurate to the melody of the songs as we all sang loudly and full throatily.

It was a powerful experience, standing on the benches and chanting in unison, "Ernesaks! Ernesaks! Ernesaks!" hoping he would lead the chorus in repeating this song. However, the Russian militia blasted march music from the enormous speakers to drown out the spontaneous singing. They assembled in force and brought out their big, leashed dogs.

A young man tried climbing up the tall tower where the flame had just been extinguished, but the Russian police apprehended him and pulled him back down. The thirty thousand singers continued singing without a conductor. The vast crowd joined them by singing along.

The shouting and singing lasted for a long while. People were reluctant to leave. They wanted to savor the feelings of unity, of connection to one another and to their heritage that the Soviets were trying to extinguish. The public also broke into singing other banned songs. This lasted for hours as groups marched along city streets. Late that night, I heard male singing groups marching through the streets near my hotel singing forbidden patriotic Estonian songs such as "*Saa Vabaks, Eesti Meri*" ("Be Free, Estonian Sea").

I had mixed joy and sadness as I slowly left the festival grounds, knowing that it would be five long years before Estonians could again experience singing with their own and not being alone.

Standing on the bench, chanting, and singing in unison with thousands of Estonians marked a massive turning point for me; from then on, I felt I must do whatever I could for my people to prevent our total annihilation.

Saa Vabaks, Eesti Meri	Be Free, Estonian Sea
Saa vabaks, Eesti meri, Saa vabaks, Eesti pind! Siis tuisku ega tormi ei karda Eesti rind.	Be free, Estonian sea; Be free, Estonian land! Through blizzards and storms, Estonian hearts will stand!

Perhaps my journey was not unlike Homer's Odysseus's quest for home following the Trojan War. Both journeys have elements of homecoming, loyalty, fate, free will and intentionality, endurance and resilience, identity, and transformation. My pursuit was set within the context of my parents' miraculous rescue at sea and the disruption of our refugee experience through life in three countries before the age of five. This may have left a lasting emotional imprint, a sense of emptiness, a hole in my soul that I sought to fill through pursuing this journey—my odyssey.

Soon after Tõnu and I took the ship back to Finland. Anni, who I had met at the Canadian Embassy in Helsinki, and Vivian, her friend, were on the dock when we returned to Helsinki in 1975, greeting us as planned. But to my utter surprise, Silja and her Finnish boyfriend Timo were there too. He was the head of the Finnish Student Organization.

Silja rushed over to me and asked if I had a necktie. She said they were taking me to a particular place, and I needed to wear a tie.

I told Tõnu to go with the ladies to Anni's place as promised, and I would come there later. I put on a tie, and we took a cab to a place down a long, dark alley. We stopped at the door to a private club. Timo had a key to get inside, and we walked in and were immediately seated. The food was fabulous. The drinks were fine. They plied me with food and drink while asking what I had done in Estonia during this current trip, who I had seen, and how my trip had been. I was stunned by being treated to such fine food at a fancy private place but wondered what was happening. I described to them my having seen relatives and how powerful the song and dance festival had been.

I didn't stay long. I told them I had promised friends we'd get together before I left for home the next day, and I needed to go. On the way to Anni's apartment, sitting alone in the cab, I kept asking myself, *What is this whole thing with Silja and Timo all about? Who is Silja, really? Why is she so interested in me?* I never did find answers to these questions.

During the cab ride to Anni's apartment, I pondered the three years between the summers of 1972 and 1975. It began with anticipation, anguish, challenge, and uncertainty when I embarked on my seven-hour journey to MÜ in Canada's Muskoka lakes and forests; the journey continued through the lakes and forests of Finland and to my trips to Estonia. I had seen my homeland for the first time, my parents' house, and felt the joy of having dinner seated at my parents' dining table from Räägu and singing old Estonian folk songs with relatives.

But there was also the ever-present odious dark cloud of the brutal occupation with its relentless Russification casting a shadow over my whole experience.

I took this photo during the singing of "*Mu Isamaa on Minu Arm.*"

The crowd leaves the song festival grounds, perhaps looking back in longing.

We are standing on the benches, shouting for Ernesaks to return.

Mu Isamaa on Minu Arm	My Homeland Is My Love
Mu isamaa on minu arm, kel südant andnud ma, sull laulan ma, mu ülem õnn, mu õitsev Eestimaa! Su valu südames mul keeb, su õnn ja rõõm mind rõõmsaks teeb, mu isamaa!	My homeland, my love, my heart belongs to you, to sing to you, my greatest joy, my flowering, my Estonia! Your pain in my heart does sear, your joy and fortune bring me joy, oh my homeland!
Mu isamaa on minu arm, ei teda jäta maa, ja peaks sada surma ma seepärast surema! Kas laimab võõra kadedus, sa siiski elad südames, mu isamaa!	My homeland, my love, never to be forsaken, though for you should I suffer death a hundred times! Even under foreign blasphemy, in my heart you remain alive, oh my homeland!
Mu isamaa on minu arm, ja tahan puhata, su rüppe heidan unele, mu püha Eestimaa! Su linnud und mull laulavad, mu põrmust lilled õitsevad, mu isamaa!	My homeland, my love, in your bosom I want to rest and dream, my sacred Estonia! Your birds sing lullabies to me, and from my ashes flowers bloom, oh my homeland!

Chapter 26

My Painting Portends: The Woman of My Dreams

The years after that summer were kind to me.

After MÜ and my trips to Finland and Estonia, where I met my relatives and attended the song festival, I realized that the most suitable option for a life partner would be an Estonian woman with whom I shared the refugee experience. Only this type of person would really understand me.

I created a clear strategy to make this happen. Because I lived in central New York State, where there were virtually no Estonians, I made it a point to attend venues and events where Estonian women would gather. I also figured that if I were the one speaking at the podium, I'd get noticed more than if I were sitting somewhere in the crowd or next to the woodwork in a corner.

I developed talks and workshops dealing with the Estonian existential reality of "marginality," the experience of living between two cultures. This was a glorious time in my life. I presented lectures and conducted workshops on these issues in Toronto, New

York City, Washington, and other places. I met many wonderful people and some lovely Estonian women.

In March 1978, I was invited to lecture at the annual Estonian Cultural Symposium in New York City. I presented two lectures on ethnic identity, one in Estonian and one in English. I also showed my 1975 Song Festival slideshow with a soundtrack before the big ball on Saturday night.

While I was preparing at the podium for the first lecture, a—I have to say it—gorgeous woman walked into the room. As she moved, she passed in front of a big hotel window, which framed her and created an iridescent angelic glow outlining her tall stature, long blond hair, and deep blue eyes. She sat directly in front of my podium.

The woman of my dreams flashed through my mind. I managed to focus on my lecture, which was well received. During the symposium, I saw her several times from afar. I couldn't approach her because I was with another woman then. I thought that maybe I'd never see her again. But a couple of months later, I was unexpectedly invited to lead talks about ethnic identity during evening campfires for older scouts and girl guides at a jamboree near Lakewood, New Jersey.

When I arrived, it was hot, muggy, and sticky. Anu, who had invited me, helped set up my tent, and then she took me to meet Kristi, the leader of the older girl guides.

And there she was. When Anu introduced us, I was shirtless, wearing only white shorts. Kristi's gaze quickly swept up and down my whole body, a good omen perhaps. She and I worked together planning the campfire discussions.

For the rest of the week, I followed her around, making myself indispensable, helping as much as possible, lifting logs, and moving things when needed. She had a background very similar to mine; her family fled in 1944, and she was born in the United States. As the week ended, we agreed that I would visit her in Willimantic, Connecticut. I could tell that she was a deeply honest, kind, generous, caring person, who was also quite smart, having just completed a master's degree.

The following week, while driving to Connecticut, thoughts of Kristi raced through my mind. My usual imagination took over, and I feared she wouldn't even be there when I arrived, along with other catastrophic thoughts.

At about noon, I slowly walked up the stairway to her apartment. I knocked, and to my relief, the door opened. My gaze moved up and down Kristi's whole body. She wore a beautiful blue evening dress and had meticulously applied makeup. Her dining table was set with a fancy meal. As we dined, she said that we would next visit her parents, who lived nearby. I sensed an intricate, delightful web closing in around me.

My visit was fantastic. As I drove home in my bright yellow Datsun 1200 (I had sold my Karmann Ghia to a colleague who loved it and then bought the Datsun), the car seemed to float above the pavement, and the scenery passed with a surreal slowness. It was like my walk along Dale Road in the summer of 1963, only now the tires floated above the road rather than my feet—but it was bliss once again.

After our wedding, her parents visited us in Utica. I was in the kitchen making dinner when I heard Kristi's mother say, "Oh, you painted a picture of Kristi!"

We were renovating, and things had been pulled out of our closet. I went into the hall and saw the painting I had done of a woman stepping out of a pure white canvas—the image I had painted on that lonely, dreary wet Sunday ten years earlier. Remarkably, it was how Kristi had looked as she was framed in the glow of the hotel window when I first saw her.

We have been married for over forty years and now have three children and five grandchildren. Our wedding day was June 28, 1980.

Chapter 27

Freedom Returns: My Homeland, My Blessing, My Joy

In the late 1980s, Soviet Premier Gorbachev's *perestroika* and *glasnost* finally lifted the sheer terror gripping people for years. Estonians soon began to hold meetings and spontaneously gathered at their song festival site. They sang long forbidden, banned songs, the singing of which had previously led many to be arrested, executed, or sent to slave labor camps. When authoritarian regimes collapse, violence often ensues. In contrast, Estonians gathered by the thousands to sing themselves free in what Heinz Valk termed the "Singing Revolution" in 1988.

The summer of 1988 witnessed a series of concerts and joint singing in Estonia, soon to turn into a large-scale popular movement and later called the Singing Revolution.

Later, in 1989, during Gorbachev's visit to the United Nations headquarters in New York, I protested. I stood on the curb and held a toy piglet with a rubber Gorbachev head attached. I carried this in a mesh bag attached to the end of a long pole. As Gorbachev drove by slowly in his black limousine, I held the mesh bag up and out into the street so he could see it.

The Russian occupation had resulted in decades of relentless, ruthless, aggressive threatening of the very existence of the Estonian people, language, and culture. The Singing Revolution of the late 1980s, when thousands spontaneously gathered to sing long-forbidden songs and wave our banned blue, black, and white flag in a massive push for freedom and independence, was essential to regaining Estonian independence.

August 1991

While visiting our good friends Tõnu and Enel (our Intourist guide in 1974 and now Tõnu's wife) in Ottawa, Ontario, we woke to Enel running down the stairs to the basement where Kristi and I were sleeping on air mattresses. She was out of breath and panting but finally stammered out that there was a coup d'état happening in Moscow.

It was Sunday morning, August 18, 1991. Enel turned on the television to CNN. We all watched the unfolding events in Moscow and throughout the Soviet Union. A friend from Estonia had telephoned Enel and told her that the Russians had blockaded all the harbors, shut down all air and rail traffic, and attacked the Estonian Television Tower with troops and tanks.

Kristi and I had just spent a week in Muskoka, Ontario, Canada, at MÜ, where I had delivered a lecture. I felt good about the positive reception of my talk. We also attended meaningful lectures, seminars, discussion groups, and a fantastic wine-tasting group each afternoon led by Eik Järvi, an official wine taster for the Liquor Control Board of Ontario (LCBO). At night, we sang well-known Estonian songs around the campfire. The Estonian historian Lauri Vahtre taught us to sing a *metsavendade laul* ("Forest Brother's

Song"). We sang it repeatedly with much glee and gusto. The seminar ended with a festive party on Friday night, August 16, 1991.

The following day we drove to the Canadian capital, Ottawa, to visit our old friends Tõnu and Enel and their sons Kristjan and Andres. We took the scenic route through Algonquin Provincial Park. In Ottawa, the Onus led us on a tour of the city and the Parliament buildings. Tõnu worked as a staffer in the Canadian Senate.

On Sunday evening, we went to bed happy and contented after a beautiful week in Muskoka and a wonderful weekend in Ottawa. We woke to the sound of Enel's shouting with the shocking news of the coup in Moscow. Groggily, we watched as the events unfolded. Gorbachev was under arrest. Troops and tanks filled the streets of Moscow, while Boris Yeltsin tried to rally the Russian people to stand up against and stop the insurrectionists.

Before this coup, events in Estonia, especially after the Singing Revolution, had filled us with hope. The years of relentless effort struggling for freedom were bearing fruit. That was suddenly at risk on this Monday morning, August 19, 1991. Our hopes for independence looked like they were evaporating before our eyes.

I called my parents in Newfane, New York. As expected, they too were distraught. Kristi and I decided that we should drive to my parents' place to be with them. Given the gravity of this crisis, we also wanted to be with our daughters, Kaili and Kiia-Mai, and especially with my parents and sisters, Helle and Tiia. It was a long drive past Toronto around the western end of Lake Ontario into the Niagara Falls area. We arrived at my parents' place in Newfane at about four thirty in the afternoon.

We struggled to understand what was happening, but one thing seemed clear: The hardline Communists who had seized power would undoubtedly crush any hope of Estonian independence. We followed the news all day on Monday, August 19, as the coup unfolded.

The next day, August 20, Kristi and I needed to go to the store. While we drove up Route 78 toward Lockport, we listened to National Public Radio. As we approached Tollgate Hill, the news came that the Estonian Supreme Soviet had just voted overwhelmingly (sixty-nine out of seventy delegates) to declare Estonian independence from the Soviet Union. It was about 4:15 in western New York; the decision in Estonia had been made at 11:03 p.m. their time. We heard the fantastic news only minutes after it happened.

The speaker of the Estonian Supreme Soviet who presided over this historic session was our relative by marriage, Ülo Nugis, my aunt Alviine's nephew—the same aunt Alviine whose husband Rudolf Nugis had been dragged from their house and shot to death by Nazi occupiers in 1941. The session was broadcast live on Estonian television. The whole country watched as Ülo struck the gavel down and declared that from that day, August 20, forward, Estonia was once again a free and independent nation.

The last Russian troops left Estonia on August 31, 1994. For Estonians, World War II finally ended on this day. President Meri negotiated over dinner this troop withdrawal with Boris Yeltsin in Moscow. Yeltsin kept filling their glasses with vodka. Lennart Meri surreptitiously poured his glasses into a planter next to him while Yeltsin got drunk. In the end, an inebriated Yeltsin signed the Russian troop withdrawal agreement. Meri later remarked, "Estonians prefer our spirits in song, not in vodka."

On August 23, the Estonian community in Rochester, New York, asked me to deliver a speech at their observance with Latvians and Lithuanians of Black Ribbon Day. I represented the Estonian American

National Council and the Estonian World Council. Black Ribbon Day marked the anniversary of the Nazi–Soviet pact in 1939, which led to the Soviet occupation of the Baltic states. This event, however, was an exciting and joyous gathering. The large turnout in downtown Rochester's Liberty Pole Plaza included my sisters Helle and Tiia, my nieces Cindy, Yvonne, and Babara, and my nephews Andres, Matti, and Ivo.

At the Rochester, New York, Black Ribbon Day demonstration.

On this beautiful day, U.S. Representative Louise Slaughter, a local member of Congress, was among the other speakers. After my speech, she hugged me and kissed me on the cheek.

On Saturday, August 24, my parents hosted a pig roast. Wade and Nelly arrived early that morning with their roasting trailer and began the process, resulting in a fabulous roasted pig by around three in the afternoon. My parents had invited many people to celebrate Estonian reindependence and the birthday of Heli Rakfeldt (Onu Arnold's wife) on August 20, 1991. Our whole family was there along with Estonian friends from the Buffalo, New York area. Additionally, my good friends from freshman year in college, John and Pat, were there.

The high point came before sitting down to dinner. We toasted with glasses of champagne to a free and independent Estonia, and all sang the Estonian national anthem. Tears of joy and from bittersweet memories streamed down the faces of many who sang.

My parents had fled Estonia on September 22, 1944, the last day of independence, as Soviet forces overran the country. Almost fifty years later, they were once again able to sing our anthem, celebrating a freedom and independence, "*Mu Isamaa, Mu õnn ja rõõm*" ("My Homeland, My Blessing, My Joy").

My *isa* (father), Ilmar, during our singing of the Estonian national anthem on August 24, 1991.

My *ema* and *isa* lighting blue, black, and white candles on August 24, 1991.

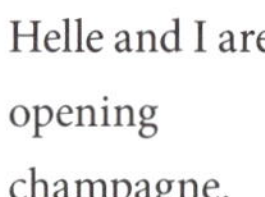

Helle and I are opening champagne.

Helle with a message on her shirt.

Singing with Kaili, Helle, Ema, and Andres.

Singing with Tiia, Helle, Kristi, Kaili, and Pat.

With my friend John from my freshman year of college, celebrating Estonian reindependence.

Mu Isamaa, Mu Õnn Rõõm	My Homeland, My Joy and Happiness
Mu isamaa, mu õnn ja rõõm, kui kaunis oled sa! Ei leia mina iial teal see suure, laia ilma peal, mis mul nii armas oleks ka, kui sa, mu isamaa!	My homeland, my greatest joy, of beauty so grand! Never will I find in the whole wide world what I cherish more than you, my homeland, my homeland!
Sa oled mind ju sünnitand ja üles kasvatand; sind tänan mina alati ja jään sull' truuiks surmani, mul kõige armsam oled sa, mu kallis isamaa!	Within you I was born and also where I grew; with eternal thanks and faithful till my dying day, you are my greatest love, my cherished homeland!
Su üle Jumal valvaku mu armas isamaa! Ta olgu sinu kaitseja ja võtku rohkest õnnista, mis iial ette võtad sa, mu kallis isamaa!	May God watch over you, my dear homeland! May He be your guardian and bring great blessings to all you may endeavor, my cherished homeland!

Chapter 28

"No One Is Alone" Sung Loudly with Thousands—Song of My Soul

Immediately after freedom and independence returned in 1991, we focused on actively lobbying for Estonia to become a member of NATO (and of the European Union) in 2004. Perhaps NATO membership will now, in 2024, save Estonia from Ukraine's fate.

A politically active global Estonian community is essential for maintaining Estonia's security. The worldwide Estonian Festivals (ESTOs), summer camps, and scouting all contribute to keeping our language, culture, and identity alive and able to be passed along to the young. However, as I have pointed out, this mission creates inner tension and conflict regarding one's identity. This internal conflict and ambivalence have caused many to eschew involvement with the exile community and their Estonian identity by melting into the American mainstream. Such a choice is understandable and should not be harshly judged. Throughout it all, the Estonian diaspora community's core goal has been to preserve the Estonian language, culture, and heritage during the relentless, brutal

Russification in Estonia. Given the uncertainties in Europe, this mission is still relevant.

In 2003, the Estonian Song and Dance Festival was recognized by UNESCO as a Masterpiece of the "Oral and Intangible Heritage of Humanity," highlighting its cultural importance. The festivals evoke strong emotions and a sense of patriotism among both participants and spectators. Singing and dancing together creates a powerful feeling of unity and national pride. The festivals have played a role in significant historical moments, including the Singing Revolution in the late 1980s, contributing to Estonia's regaining independence from the Soviet Union.

As a family, we have continued to attend the huge Estonian song festivals. Kristi, our son Jaak Kristjan, and I attended in 2019. The experience was emotionally and aesthetically powerful. As we walked down the middle of Narva Maantee, after the first night of the festival, along with thousands of other attendees, back toward the center of Tallinn, the warm twilight glow of the midnight sky enveloped us. Through the din of the talking, the laughter, and the singing, I heard someone behind me calling my name: "Jaak, Jaak."

I turned to see Kristi's cousin, Anne, running toward me, smiling, with her arms outstretched. We hadn't seen each other for more than twenty years. I asked how she had recognized me from behind among all these people. She said that she knew it was me when she heard my voice. Kristi and Anne embraced. We stood in the middle of the street, discussing our lives during the decades since we last met.

This unexpected encounter also led to our meeting with Anne's two sisters, Heidi and Made, Anne's daughter Marika, and Kristi's half-sister, Tiiu, whom she hadn't seen for many years.

We agreed to get together with other members of Kristi's family at a restaurant near our hotel. There, Tiiu described her vivid memory of the last time she saw their father, Elmar, in the early 1940s. He had come home late one night from the battlefront and implored his wife to escape to the West in the morning with him. But Tiiu's mother would not leave her family, friends, and homeland. She refused to go with him. So, Elmar fled, leaving behind his three-year-old daughter Tiiu and his wife.

Kristi's mother Maimo fled in September 1944 with her two sisters, Aino and Hilja, and her three-year-old son, Jaak. Their husbands had all urged them to escape while the men stayed behind to defend their homeland. But Maimo and her sisters never saw their husbands again. They all died in battle.

They managed to get on a ship that got them through Poland to Germany, where the women were taken into custody and forced to work at a German munitions factory near Berlin. Kristi's older half-brother Jaak described at our dinner how as a three-and-a-half-year-old he watched the Allies' relentless bombing of Berlin. When not hunkered down in a bomb shelter, he could feel the heat from the burning city several miles away.

When the war ended, Maimo and her family went to Geslingen in the U.S. sector in southern Germany. The Allies had removed Germans from their homes and squeezed multiple Estonian families into often small living spaces. Thousands of other Estonian refugees were housed there. They quickly created a vibrant cultural life. They organized schools, sports events, concerts, religious congregations, and song and dance festivals. Here in this displaced-person camp, Maimo met and married Elmar, who had left his family behind and never saw them again. After the Displaced Persons Act became law, they could come to America, where Kristi was born in Hartford, Connecticut.

Thousands of Estonians fled the Russian invasion in the fall of 1944. In 2022, I delivered a speech in Estonian at the Parliamentary Conference Hall. In my speech, I strongly urged Parliament to designate an annual day of remembrance for those who fled and for those who died while attempting to do so.

The 2019 Song Festival was titled "My Love" ("*Minu Arm*"). The homophone "arm" in Estonian means both "love" and "scar." Estonians carry traumatic scars from the horrors and brutality experienced during much of the twentieth century. However, they have healed as a people through singing together and feeling a deep connection to each other and their homeland.

Before meeting Kristi's relatives, we had sung together at the 2019 Song Festival in perfect unison with hundreds of thousands of Estonians, performing the call-and-response folk melody: "*Üksi pole keegi, üksi pole keegi.*" ("No one is alone, no one is alone.") Standing in the middle of the wide boulevard, surrounded by thousands of others embracing, talking, and connecting with Kristi's long-lost family members, we were truly filled with the warmth and joy of not being alone.

As we walked back to our hotel along the broad boulevard, my thoughts filled with the night in 1972 when I returned from my first MÜ to my ragged, funky student apartment in Syracuse, with its four-by-four-foot raw, unfinished piece of plywood set onto cinder blocks in the middle of the living room, which served as my coffee table. Sitting in my ragged old chair, I had found solace by embracing my guitar. I was looking at my painting of my dream woman. The epiphany was my realization that perhaps having such an Estonian woman in my life, with whom I could share our obscure, arcane language, historical roots, cultural traditions, and the painful injustice of the brutal occupation, could allow me to deepen my connection with my community of the worldwide Estonian diaspora—one immersive week in Muskoka had already begun to fill that empty place in my soul.

That night, in Syracuse, after my return from Canada, I had assuaged my loneliness and emptiness by playing my guitar and softly singing Estonian folk songs while looking at the painting of my dream woman. And now, here I was in Estonia, with my dream woman at my side along with our son. We had just reconnected with family. We had just sung with thousands of others the call-and-response folk melody promising no one is alone. It connected me not just to the land and its people but also to the enduring spirit of my ancestors. Singing this song was a moment of unity, which was transformative, reminding me of our shared humanity, striving to fulfill our hopes and dreams with the power of song to heal and uplift.

The empty hole in my soul had been filled, and my quest, journey, and odyssey had brought me to this fulfilling place. As I walked down the street, a broad smile spread across my face, overflowing with satisfaction, warmth, and a connection to our ancient, mystical Estonian culture and its people, who have inhabited this small land along the Baltic Sea for thousands of years. This connection emerged as I sang loudly with thousands of others the song "No One Is Alone," my unique song of my soul.

The lead singer in the song "*Üksi pole keegi*" ("No") ("No One Is Alone") in a call-and-response format.

The next photos show the size of the audience at the song festival all singing together.

Kristi and I sang along with thousands of others.

Üksi Pole Keegi	No One Is Alone
üksi pole keegi. Keskel häid ja, keskel häid ja omaseid, üksi pole, üksi pole keegi	No one is alone. In midst of good, in midst of good with one's own, no one is alone, no one is alone.

Acknowledgments

I thank Laura Matthews for her exceptional structuring and editing of the extensive material I had written over the years. I had planned to write a description of my parents, the Estonian people, and our family's journey to the West, but Laura strongly encouraged me to become the focal point of the piece. This was extremely difficult at first, but it proved to be the right approach. I'm indebted to Laura's talent and creativity.

My membership in Dr. John Strauss's writing group at Yale has been a significant part of this process. This group provided a safe venue for me to write many pieces that appear in the book. I thank Dr. Strauss and all the members of the group for their support, encouragement, and valuable feedback.

I am blessed with friends who read earlier sections and drafts of the manuscript, providing me with excellent feedback and continual encouragement. Among these individuals are Keith and Susan Corneau, Michael and Jeanne Leonard, Richard Lesser,

Tõnu Onu, George Strong, and Sharon Benedetto. Additionally, Hando Nahkur assisted with the song lyrics. My publishing team was outstanding. In particular, I would like to thank CW Patrick, who served as my project manager and did an excellent job.

I am fortunate to have loving and supportive children, Kaili, Kiia-Mai, and Jaak Kristjan. Jaak Kristjan also helped overcome and resolve various complex technical issues.

Most significantly, I thank my wife, Kristi, to whom I am deeply grateful for her love, support, and constant encouragement throughout the years I spent working on this project.

About the Author

Jaak Rakfeldt, PhD, is a Professor Emeritus at Southern Connecticut State University, where he was the coordinator of the Co-occurring Disorders Cohort Program (mental health and substance use). In addition, he has been an assistant clinical professor at the Yale University School of Medicine Department of Psychiatry. For several years, he has provided clinical supervision for third-year psychiatry residents. Dr. Rakfeldt has served as a clinical consultant and conducted seminars and colloquia at various community mental health agencies. He has published over sixty papers and chapters and given over one hundred conference presentations. He also has maintained a private clinical practice. Dr. Rakfeldt has been a member of the Estonian American National Council, the Estonian World Council, and the Estonian Academic Fraternity-Korp! Fraternitas Estica, and the chairman of the Connecticut Estonian Society.

He has also published in the area of Estonian identity issues, which includes the following:

Rakfeldt, J. (1978). Äärel Olemine: Kahe Kultuuri ja Ühiskonna Vahel (Life at the Edge Between Two Cultures and Societies). *Ajakiri, 4*, 26–31.

Rakfeldt, J. (1984). Eesti Noored ja Sümboolne Suhtlemisteooria Marginaalsuses (Young Estonians and Symbolic Interaction Theory Related to the Issue of Marginality). *Metsaülikool 1967–1982*, (pp. 131–135). Toronto, Ontario: Kotkajärve Metsaülikool and the Ontario Ministry of Citizenship and Culture.

Rakfeldt, J. (1993). Põhja-Ameerika Eestlaste Identsusest (Estonian-American Ethnic Identity Issues). *Akadeemia, 5*(1), 3–12.

Rakfeldt, J., & Rakfeldt-Leetmaa, H. (1996). Rahvusliku Identiteedi Säilitamine Okupeeritud Eestis (The Preservation of Ethnic Identity in Occupied Estonia). *Akadeemia, 8*(8), 1571–1590.

Rakfeldt, J. (2012). *Eesti Noorte Identiteet* (Ethnic Identity among Younger Estonians) in T. Kirss (ed)., *Metsaülikool 1983–2005* (pp. 49–59). Kotkajärve Metsaülikool, A.S. Uniprint.

Rakfeldt, J. (2015). *Kodust lahkumine* (Flight from Home). *Looming, 5*, 671–675.

Rakfeldt, J. (2015). Home Environments, Memories, and Life Stories: Preservation of Estonian National Identity. *Journal of Baltic Studies, 46*(4), 511–542.